MW01039621

Ask Amy

ADVICE FOR BETTER LIVING

AMY DICKINSON

MIDWAY
AN AGATE IMPRINT
CHICAGO

Chicago Tribune

Tony W. Hunter, Publisher

Gerould W. Kern, Editor

R. Bruce Dold, Editorial Page Editor

Bill Adee, Senior Vice President/Digital

Jane Hirt, Managing Editor

Joycelyn Winnecke, Associate Editor

Peter Kendall, Deputy Managing Editor

Printed in the United States of America

Library of Congress Cataloging-in-Publication Data

Dickinson, Amy.

 Ask Amy : advice for better living / Amy Dickinson.

   pages cm

 Includes index.

 Summary: "A collection of excerpts from the syndicated advice column "Ask Amy""-- Provided by publisher.

 ISBN 978-1-57284-155-0 (pbk.) -- ISBN 1-57284-155-9 (pbk.) -- ISBN 978-1-57284-461-2 (ebook) -- ISBN 1-57284-461-2 (ebook)

 1. Interpersonal relations--Psychological aspects. I. Title.

 BF1045.I58D53 2013

 070.4'44--dc23

                              2013031513

10 9 8 7 6 5 4 3 2 1

Midway is an imprint of Agate Publishing. Agate books are available in bulk at discount prices. For more information visit agatepublishing.com.

Table of Contents

· · · · · · · · · · · · · · · · · · · ·

Introduction

• •

DEAR READERS: In 2002, the Chicago Tribune lost a legend when the irreplaceable Ann Landers (real name, Eppie Lederer) died at the age of 83. In 47 years of writing her column, Landers cemented her place in American life. Her daily advice column influenced lawmakers, leaders and regular people by serving up the truth—often with a side of sass.

After Landers' death, the Tribune undertook a national search to find another columnist to somehow try to replace Ann Landers, while honoring her legacy.

They found me. At the time, I was an unemployed writer with a career history as a television producer, radio reporter and editor, and a more recent stint as a columnist for *Time* magazine. Most importantly, I was a single mother raising my daughter as I strung together freelance gigs so I could work from home.

After an audition process that resembled a Ginger Rogers musical ("Quick, the star broke her ankle!"), I was chosen to try to create a new version of a very old genre. My daughter and I moved from Washington, D.C., to Chicago, and I got to work.

It has been more than 10 years since the "Ask Amy" column debuted in the Chicago Tribune, and it has since been syndicated across the country. In that time, my daily column has been the home to thousands of questions submitted from readers on every imaginable topic—including several topics that I never knew existed. The defining characteristic of every column is that it contains an honest query about human behavior.

I answer these questions by myself—no, I don't have a staff, as many readers assume. I read the incoming mail myself, choose which questions to publish and approach my answers with all the wisdom, compassion and wit (with a side of sass) that I can muster. I am not a professional psychologist, physician or member of the clergy. I'm a regular person with an extraordinary interest in human behavior. I research trends, read studies, talk to people and interview experts. But the most important research I bring to my column is the wisdom I've gathered by living my life out in the world.

In the last 10 years I've experienced my own personal loss, sadness, depression and periods of uncertainty. I raised one child and then acquired several more five years ago when I married a childhood friend. My life is one of challenges, punctuated by pleasure, laughter, uncertainty and many, many moments of joy. In short, my life is very much like the lives of those readers who write to "Ask Amy" for advice, and also like the hundreds of people who contact me each day through email, Twitter, Facebook and good, old-fashioned U.S. mail to say they read the column.

I hope you enjoy this collection of recent questions and answers, chosen by editors of the Tribune to represent my recent work. They have helpfully sorted the Q-and-A into topics. But remember this: Most of human behavior doesn't fall into neat categories. True wisdom resides between definitive answers. The most I hope to do for my readers is give them a space to tell their story, as well as a respectful ear and an answer that I hope they will apply to their own lives in a positive way.

Amy Dickinson
2013
TWITTER: @askingamy
FACEBOOK: ADickinsonDaily
EMAIL: askamy@tribune.com

Marriage

....

For Better, for Worse — and Not
Necessarily Forever

Coping with a lazy, jobless husband

DEAR AMY: I am a 21-year-old married woman, working at an internship and attending college full time to finish my associate degree. I am very busy.

My husband was laid off about eight months ago, and because of this we had to move in with my parents. I've been trying to be the supportive wife as much as I can be, but things are becoming more challenging and stressful.

I come home from a busy day to find dishes in the sink and dirty laundry on the floor, and I end up having to cook and clean all night. I'm beginning to lose hope that he will ever find a job. Furthermore, I don't think he is even looking anymore.

I'm beginning to resent him. I question whether I even want to stay married to him. I've tried giving him ultimatums and have tried being supportive at the same time. I feel as if I am becoming the nagging wife I always told myself I wouldn't be, but I just don't know what else to do. How do I save my marriage from a financial hiccup like this?

— *Nagging Wife*

DEAR WIFE: A hiccup is a temporary glitch. If things don't change, this could be a way of life. Ultimatums don't work if there is no real consequence attached. If your marriage is on the line, then say so.

In a healthy, functioning marriage both partners do a lifetime dance — and they switch or share roles when they need to. You two should sit down when you are not in the midst of a stressful maelstrom and talk about expectations and efforts.

Is your husband willing to have the housework done by 4 p.m. each day? Is he willing to hustle to mow lawns or wash windows to keep busy and bring in some cash? And if not, why not? After your schooling and professional training, are you willing to go to work full time to support the two of you?

In addition to being helpful to the household (and respecting your parents' home), stepping up will make your husband feel energized and useful — and will help with his job search.

Wife says no to starring in peep show

DEAR AMY: My husband and I have been married for more than 30 years. This year for Christmas we received a great little video camera. You can imagine my surprise when, after some holiday cheer followed by some holiday "whoopee," he disclosed that he had hidden the camera and filmed our sexual encounter. I was furious.

I went along with some of this stuff years ago, but it didn't diminish the requests. I thought we had settled this issue in a marriage counselor's office, when I asserted that I was not into this sort of photojournalism. The counselor encouraged me to be very clear — and for him to understand that no means no.

I try to be cheerful or playful when my husband brings this up, but I also say it makes me uncomfortable. His response is, "What does it hurt?" Am I being overly sensitive, or does this grandmother have a right to say what she wants to do with her body?

— *Perplexed*

DEAR PERPLEXED: When your husband secretly shoots video of you and then asks, "What does it hurt?" your answer is, "Me. It hurts me."

In a balanced marriage, that should be enough. You have discussed his peep show porn habit before, and you have stated that "no means no." Try again.

Because this statement may be too subtle for him, you could attach a consequence to it, by conveying that this makes you so uncomfortable that it diminishes your desire to be intimate. There might be a way for you to compromise to share an experience he considers sexually thrilling and you find fulfilling — or at least, not demeaning.

Weight gain tips scales in this marriage

DEAR AMY: I am an active, physically fit 42-year-old man. I have always been an active person and married a lady 10 years ago who at the time was in shape and active too. Over time, my 40-year-old wife has lost interest in things we used to do together. She has gained 50 pounds over the past couple of years. She's the same great lady I fell in love with, but I am no longer sexually attracted to her.

Don't waste your breath with the "shallow" lecture — I understand that. But the fact remains that her weight is a sexual problem for me. Would counseling help me? I love her, but I want a rewarding sex life also.

— Shallow in Denver

DEAR SHALLOW: Because you have self-identified as "shallow," I will proclaim you to be otherwise. Shallow is: "You're fat. I don't love you because you're fat. I'm leaving you to be a backup dancer for Beyonce." That's not you. You are also overly generous (perhaps) to assume that counseling for you will somehow cure your physical aversion.

Your wife has lost interest in activities that she used to enjoy. She put on a lot of weight in a relatively short amount of time. My armchair analysis is that she may have a medical problem, and you should encourage her to see a physician to have a thorough checkup. She may have undiagnosed thyroid problems, depression or myriad other issues.

Beyond that, marriage counseling will help you both communicate about this, and to do so in a way that is kind and compassionate and with respectful regard to your sexual desires — and your relationship. If couples counseling isn't helping, you could see a therapist with expertise in dealing with men at midlife.

Dental issue sets wife's teeth on edge

DEAR AMY: This is a very delicate situation, but I need your help. My husband has really bad teeth.

I knew this before we married, so it's not a new situation. Even though his teeth are in terrible shape, if he brushes them like normal people his breath is at least acceptable. Unfortunately for me, he only brushes them once a day.

In the past I've talked to him about brushing more often, and for a while he does, but he has gone back to the once-a-day routine. His breath is unbearable. What do I do?

— Nauseated

DEAR NAUSEATED: If your spouse won't tell you you have bad breath, then who will? It might be easier if you didn't feel this was so delicate. You are married to someone who has a problem that affects you — and possibly people outside your household. His problem is fairly easily solved by more frequent brushing — unlike some people, who have chronically bad breath.

You should tell him, "I know we talked about this before, but your breath is really strong. I really wish you would brush twice a day, honey. I can tell it makes a real difference when you do."

Make sure you have plenty of dental rinse and other supplies on hand. Help him to establish a healthier habit and let him know when he succeeds.

Wife's inability to let go makes husband want to

DEAR AMY: My wife and I got married four months ago. It is the second marriage for both of us after many years alone. We are in our early 50s. I have spent the last six months discarding household items to make space in my home for her. I emptied out the master bedroom and bathroom so that she could have ample room for her things.

It is now total chaos. It makes me feel uneasy to go into that room. There's mismatched furniture in odd places and piles of laundry stacked on every available surface, including the bed. It bothers me so much that I've moved into the guest bedroom. I also spend a lot of time trying to pick up the rest of the house.

My wife seems unable to discard, pack and move from her house into mine. Her house is full of broken/mismatched furniture, piles of papers and mail, old TVs, etc. She has things in her kitchen pantry that have 8-year-old expiration dates marked on them.

I had hoped that she could work through it, but it's not happening. What can I do to help her?

— *Frustrated*

DEAR FRUSTRATED: You may not be able to help your wife without professional assistance. Whether or not she is a hoarder in the strictest sense, her anxiety concerning her possessions will continue to affect your relationship until she gets help to break through her paralysis.

You could both be inspired by reading, "Enough Already!: Clear the Emotional and Mental Clutter to Create the Life You Want" by organization expert Peter Walsh (2009, Free Press).

If your wife continues to have trouble with this process, therapy will help her identify her issues and treat her anxiety.

Pot smoking causes premarital strife

DEAR AMY: I've been engaged for about six months, and we're getting ready to start planning our wedding. We have a great relationship and I am very excited to spend the rest of my life with him. I have no complaints about my fiancé, except that he wants to start smoking marijuana when he's with his friends. He sees his friends twice a year or so, because they live elsewhere.

I am absolutely not OK with the idea of him smoking marijuana. I think he's going to jeopardize our great (and drug-free) relationship, but he doesn't see smoking marijuana as being "bad." He sees it as similar to drinking a beer. I completely disagree and I can't think of a way to compromise.

I told him I will not marry him if he chooses to smoke with his friends, but I would be willing to continue to date him. He says I'm placing conditions on marriage.

I don't know what to do. We are crazy about each other, but this "debate" about drugs has left me devastated. It never seems to be resolved.

— *Straight-laced*

DEAR STRAIGHT: One difference between smoking pot and drinking beer is that it is (still) illegal to smoke marijuana. From what you say above, marijuana doesn't sound all that important to your fiancé in the first place; so you should assume that this issue is a placeholder for other things. Control, for instance.

Because you two are at an impasse, you should step away from this issue altogether. You have stated your case, you will not change your mind, and he, evidently, won't either. He is right — you are placing conditions on marriage. He is, too.

If you decide to go the marriage route, you two should definitely pursue premarital counseling. A counselor will identify tension points between you and help you to mediate this — and other — issues so they won't become ultimatums.

Husband brings on the jokes; wife is not amused

DEAR AMY: My husband likes to joke about how much I'm eating. He thinks it's funny and frankly can't understand why I get offended by his jokes. I'm in great shape, but really it's not even about that. Last night he made a joke after analyzing some bills. He said, "Wow, you are voracious!"

I'm pregnant with our first child, we are both happy to be parents, but these jokes make me feel bad. I tried to explain that (like most women) somewhere deep in my soul I worry about my weight, so I don't want to hear such jokes — especially now when I'm gaining baby weight.

Should I eat less just to give him an impression that I'm not voracious?! I don't think so. But how can I explain to him that such hints and jokes hurt me?

— *Good Eater*

DEAR EATER: You've already explained to your husband how these jokes affect you, and either he doesn't understand or doesn't care. I agree that this is insensitive, but I suggest that you let it lie. Let it lie, like a chocolate glazed Dunkin' Donut. And don't touch it.

If you let it lie and he continues making inappropriate jokes at your expense, you can respond by saying, "Honey, I know it's scary to have a baby. I have a feeling you're making jokes because you're nervous about it. So go ahead and tell me what you're really thinking. Are you worried about my getting fat? Are you worried about the expense?"

Couple wins lottery, loses perspective

DEAR AMY: I have lived with a man for 10 years. He had a great job but lost it after many years because of an indiscretion. He has refused to find any meaningful employment since then. He has never gone outside of the "box" and doesn't seem to have much imagination or sense of adventure.

Good fortune has come recently because of a lottery win, and now the two of us are self-sufficient. Prior to this win, I was very content with my life and my seasonal position. I wish to continue this scenario for the next couple of years. (I am 57 years old.) This job has kept me in contact with the outside world and always gives me a sense of accomplishment.

My "spouse," on the other hand, indicates that he wants me to give this all up in order to accompany him in his daily life because he has no "life" of his own. I continue to encourage him to do his own thing on occasion but have had difficulty in doing so. Any suggestions?

— *Lottery Winner*

DEAR WINNER: From your description, you seem to be the one inside the "box," and frankly, that's a good thing. Lottery winners do best when they don't make any drastic moves. The most successful winners hold on to their jobs, homes and relationships — and use their windfall to achieve and sustain long-term financial stability.

You both are in a wonderful position to achieve a nice balance in life — between work and leisure, travel and home. You should both receive professional financial counseling — because you may not have a realistic view of how far your winnings will take you.

You also need to conduct a big picture discussion about your ideas and ideals. You should each declare an individual goal and then name a goal you would ideally like to share with your partner. Your goal might be to continue working for the next two years; his might be to stay home and tinker.

Then you each get to choose an experience the other will share — but you are not responsible for providing him with constant company. He'll have to make the most of his good fortune.

She wants intimacy; he wants television

DEAR AMY: I am 51, and my husband is 63. We've been married a little over a year, and there is no physical intimacy. He's talked to his doctor (briefly), and his testosterone is normal. But his favorite thing to do is sit on the couch after dinner and watch TV until 2 a.m. Then he comes to bed. On the rare occasions when he's in bed before 10, he's reading with the TV on.

When I ask to kiss or snuggle, he exhales deeply with such an annoyed look — while at the same time slamming his book on his lap. I am starving for physical intimacy. We've started seeing a counselor, but nothing seems to be working.

— *Lonely Wife*

DEAR LONELY: Your counselor should suggest ways for you to compromise on how you spend your time. Sharing hobbies and experiences outside of (and at) home will help draw you closer. If you aren't physically active, you and your husband would both benefit from regular exercise, individually and together. Getting the television out of your bedroom will also help.

This is assuming your husband really wants to be in this marriage with you. You should not have to ask him to kiss or cuddle. Affection is not a favor to be bestowed, and testosterone should not affect your husband's desire to express warmth and affection — unless he is afraid that it will lead to a sexual encounter he is not willing (or able) to have.

Talking paves the way toward intimacy. Use your sessions with your counselor to learn new ways to talk — and listen — to each other.

Sex-starved husband wants bed partner

DEAR AMY: I have been happily married for 35 years and still love my wife. However, 12 years ago, when she went through menopause, she lost all interest in sex. She didn't just lose interest, but felt repulsed by it.

Before that we had a happy sex life. She has seen medical specialists, tried medications and psychiatry, but nothing has helped.

Meanwhile, my desires have only multiplied through frustration since I have been true to her and have not wanted to hurt her by going outside our marriage for sexual fulfillment.

However, after a dozen years of this I have reached the end of my tolerance, and all I think about is sex. Because there is an expectation in marriage of sexual fulfillment, am I wrong to consider going outside my marriage for relief?

I know I would suggest this to my wife if the roles were reversed, but I also know she would be devastated if she found out I was going to another woman for sexual release. I can't go on like this.

— *Frustrated*

DEAR FRUSTRATED: I can imagine that this is not only sexually frustrating, but also heartbreaking for both of you. You say your wife has tried remedies for her sexual aversion, but you don't mention any efforts you have made to address this as a couple. You also don't mention your own individual effort — aside from the idea that you would look outside your marriage for sexual fulfillment.

The good news is that your wife seems to be open to addressing this problem. This is a problem the two of you share, however, and your marriage is at risk.

You two should see a therapist who has expertise in working with couples about sexual issues. An experienced therapist will not be thrown off by your wife's aversion and your response, and will coach both of you with a goal of reviving your sexual connection.

There are many books offering some perspective on this fairly common problem. One I like is "The Sex-Starved Marriage: A Couple's Guide to Boosting Their Marriage Libido," by Michele Weiner-Davis (Simon & Schuster, 2003).

Finding long-lost relative is bittersweet

DEAR AMY: My husband has two children from a previous marriage and an older child from a very brief marriage before that, when he was in his early 20s.

Although he is a great dad to his two youngest, when we met, he shamefully admitted that he hadn't seen or spoken to his oldest child in several years and desperately wanted to reconnect with her. I strongly encouraged him to do so.

Months turned into years, and he never contacted her.

Then, a few years ago, the girl's mother wrote with their new address. He seemed genuinely excited about the prospect of talking to his daughter again, but we lost the envelope containing the address.

Out of the blue, I managed to find the girl on a social networking site.

I explained who I was and out of respect for her, I told her I would not inform her father of my discovery unless she gave me her blessing first.

She was very gracious and said she appreciated my thoughtfulness. She also politely informed me that she had no desire to speak to or get to know her father in any way. She felt that he had broken too many promises and missed too many opportunities in the past.

Although it saddens me greatly, I wish to respect her decision.

She has declined to provide any further contact info, and I expect that she'll be "unfriending" me soon.

My husband has no idea that I found her. Should I stop encouraging him so much? Should I tell him everything? Should I not say anything and hope that he finds her on his own?

He feels bad enough, so he is better off just not knowing?

— *Wondering Wife*

DEAR WONDERING: Do not let his paralysis create an atmosphere of secrecy between you. Tell your husband what you've done. I think his daughter's reaction to this contact is completely natural, and he should understand that she is as stuck as he is.

The ex-wife chose to notify your husband of her new address for a reason. The same social network that led you to this daughter would also lead your husband to his ex-wife, who should be able to broker some sort of contact between the two.

The huge emotional weight he carries will ease the minute he makes any effort. Your job should be to encourage and support his efforts, not to do this for him.

Future husband not love of her life

DEAR AMY: I am a 25-year-old woman and I am engaged to a wonderful man. I have had other serious relationships and have been in love before.

My problem is that I do not love my fiancé as much as I have loved my ex-boyfriend. I can't pinpoint the reason. My fiancé is wonderful, and I do love him very much, and I know he will be an excellent husband.

I can never be with my ex ever again, so should I go through with the wedding? Will I eventually forget about my ex?

— *Worried Fiancée*

DEAR WORRIED: You may not forget about your ex. In fact, your feelings about your ex may grow more intense with time, depending on the pressures and anxieties brought on by your other relationships.

Because you are aware of this issue before your marriage, you should do everything possible to understand and resolve these feelings before you marry. This issue is best handled with a professional counselor. A therapist can listen to your story and through careful questioning, help you to understand your motivations and reactions.

Once you understand more about who you were when you were in this previous relationship, you can start to put it in perspective.

It is not necessary to quantify love; instead you should pay close attention and try to understand the qualities of your various attachments and relationships.

Husband's hanky grosses out wife

DEAR AMY: My wife and I have been married for 51 years, and we have been able to resolve most of our differences — with one notable exception.

I was brought up to always have a handkerchief on me. My wife claims that it is disgusting and unhygienic to put all those germs into your pockets. I say it is better than sniffing, snorting, wiping your nose on your sleeve or blowing a hole in a tissue — plus you waste a great deal of paper.

This discussion is now spanning three generations, and we need a resolution.

— Charles

DEAR CHARLES: I've always believed that you know you're dealing with a "gentleman" when he pulls a cloth handkerchief out of his pocket.

On the other hand, the alternative to carrying a handkerchief should not be wiping your nose on your sleeve.

Most important, the fact that this is the primary issue over which you and your wife disagree means that your marriage is an exceptional one.

Three's a crowd in this marriage

DEAR AMY: My husband very strongly dislikes my best friend. He feels that she is a "bad influence" on me, as she is still dating and hasn't settled down in her late 20s, goes to a gym that offers "pole fitness" classes, and had an abortion a year ago.

He also knows that I confide in her when he and I have a bad fight or I when I need to vent about something relating to our relationship. She and I have known each other since we were in elementary school. She is always very supportive, and I try to be there for her.

I am relatively newly wed and love my husband, but relationships are hard, and I feel justified in having someone to talk to about problems I cannot always discuss with him. He is always angry when I am talking to her on the phone and has gone so far as to hack into my email account and read our emails to each other.

My friend does not harbor any ill will toward him, but she is frank about her concerns that he can be controlling at times. I hate having him sulking and angry, but I feel I should be able to chat privately with my friend. We have been there for each other through a lot of difficult times and share a lot of similar views on life.

— Conflicted

DEAR CONFLICTED: Your husband is being unreasonable. But then, so are you. The problem here is that you are putting your friendship with your girlfriend in the middle of your relationship with your husband. You also need to learn how to dole out information like a grown-up.

Why, for instance, would you tell your husband that your girlfriend had an abortion (I'm assuming you shared this with him)? And why are you confiding in her about private matters in your marriage?

Your behavior invites each of these people to harshly judge the other — because you are sharing essentially private and/or negative information with each of them. You don't seem to have done anything to bring them together, and most of your behavior keeps them separate.

You three need a do-over. You should be able to "chat privately" with your friend, but you should also welcome your husband into the circle from time to time. And he needs to grow up too.

His porn habit gives wife a fantasy

DEAR AMY: My husband and I are in our 60s and have been to three therapists in the 25 years we've been together. Inevitably he charms the therapists (all were women), and they allow him to talk on and on about himself. I try to assert myself, eventually get fed up and quit. So now, I am in therapy on my own.

My husband has always enjoyed Playboy and similar magazines. These drive me nuts. I feel they degrade women. Now he has begun looking at porn online. I'm enraged. When I walk in on him and see him doing this, I can't breathe for a day. I fantasize about getting away from him forever.

My therapist implies that this is normal male behavior and that I should avoid walking in on him by calling out in advance or by knocking. Can you think of ways to help me?

— *Distraught*

DEAR DISTRAUGHT: Even though viewing pornography is increasingly common (due to easy access on the Internet), I disagree with your therapist that this is "normal male behavior." However, your husband has established that this is "normal" for him.

In addition to other legitimate concerns (such as the dehuman-izing view of women), pornography desensitizes people to actual (versus virtual) sexual experiences. I read a study recently showing how repeated viewing of pornography affects the chemistry of a per-son's brain, creating a "high" that is increasingly hard to duplicate in "real" life.

This is insidious and damaging — as porn replaces partners. If you can't mediate this and you continue to feel like a second-class citi-zen in your marriage, your other option is to make your own fantasy a reality.

Damsels in distress bring on wife's distress

DEAR AMY: My husband and I have been married for seven years. In his prior relationships, he was attracted to what I would call "help-less women." I have never been helpless and don't know how to be.

A few months ago, he met someone through his job who fits the "helpless and needy" description. I recently found out that he was spending several hours a week on his cellphone at work talking with her and checking on her "to make sure she was OK and wouldn't harm herself."

I confronted both of them, separately, face to face. I believe him when he says it was just conversation, but after knowing this man for 20-plus years, I don't trust him. What happens next time he meets a damsel in distress?

— *Wondering Wife*

DEAR WIFE: Rather than policing, confronting and controlling your husband and his damsels, you should expend some effort talking calmly with him about these relationships and their effect on you.

It will be necessary for you to clarify and articulate what about this bothers you so much. Do you think your husband has poor taste in people? Do you feel threatened? Are you nervous that he will get en-snared in a drama you don't trust him to handle? Would you be less bothered if the damsel were a dude?

Finding words to help needy writer

DEAR AMY: My husband desperately wants to be a famous published author. I edited his book numerous times before it got "published" online, and now he is writing stories on the Web that he hopes to compile into a novel. He expects me to edit all of these stories.

Being his editor before was awful. Although he fixed what I suggested and I helped him make the writing tighter, he didn't learn and the same mistakes occurred over and over again. He can't seem to edit or analyze his own writing.

I pulled back from editing because of my demanding full-time job. I am still expected to read everything he writes, and I struggle. First, I am confronted by all those mistakes.

Second, I am confronted by his needy questions: "Did you like this?" "Did you like that?" "What did you think about that event?" "Was it good?" It goes on and on.

He has participated in writing groups but left them. He took a writing class, but he had conflicts with the instructor — an award-winning author. He yearns for my approval. He craves my adoring accolades. And he is driving me nuts. Advice?

— *Exhausted Wife*

DEAR EXHAUSTED: It is important for spouses to know that their partners are on their side. But it is also important for your husband to realize that demanding your praise makes you hostile toward him and his creative projects.

And so you say to him, "I am your biggest fan. But I don't love every single thing you write." Your husband should hire an editor/assistant to help him. His writing would improve if an objective party could give him suggestions and directives. If he hired someone, he might value these suggestions enough to follow them because he would be paying for them.

But we both know he won't take suggestions. He wants to cut corners without improving his work; he also wants the fame along with the accolades from you. In short, he sounds like every needy, unpublished and eager writer I know.

Some spouses can write and edit together, but for many couples who are not Virginia and Leonard Woolf, these two roles don't always mix well. Your adoring accolades will mean nothing if you are not honest. Without honesty, the empty praise will bring on more insecurity.

Talk to him about his work, and expect him to talk with you about yours.

Woman wants to be runaway bride

DEAR AMY: I attended a very religious university where 50 percent of the student body is married before they graduate. I succumbed to the societal pressure and got married during my senior year. Now, at 22, I have been married for 11 months and am very unhappy. I no longer have any personal friends, and every dollar I earn is disappearing to pay for his graduate school.

My husband is a wonderful person, we do not fight and have similar interests, but I married him after knowing him for only six months and do not love him. I want to be independent and have my own life where I can concentrate on my own career and social life.

I desperately want a divorce. I want to end this marriage before any children or property complicates it, but I am so scared of the shame and reactions from our conservative families. I keep thinking that I should simply "run away" and cut off all contact from my family and his, so all the blame for the separation can be put on me, but I know that is not the mature solution.

My whole life I have been afraid to step on the toes of my conservative family and peers. I don't see their religion to be rational, so why should I be rational now?

— *Wannabe Runaway*

DEAR WANNABE: Because this is a persistent fantasy for you, you should put the concept of running away in your back pocket, as something you would do only after you've tried everything else (including trying to make your marriage work).

Choose to behave with integrity. Don't blame your husband, whom you describe as a wonderful person. Well, if he is wonderful, then allow him to be wonderful to you by discussing this issue honestly.

You should explore this carefully. Seek out the counsel of someone who is older, wiser, understanding, supportive and sympathetic. See family pressure for what it is — an expression of desperation on the part of people who cannot ultimately live your life for you.

Happy couple's perfect aphrodisiac

DEAR AMY: Can a sexless marriage last? My wife and I have been married for 17 years and our sex life has been slowing down for a long time. If I averaged our sexual encounters throughout the years they would number no more than 10 times a year.

My wife and I get along great and we are best friends. She is very attractive and fun to be with, but I don't know what happened to us. The strange part is that we are more friends than lovers. What causes women to lose their sex drive? There are no medical reasons for this. Then they wonder why their husbands have an affair!

I don't think it's another man. I do want a fun and active sex life and I am starting to wonder if maybe I can have this with the right person who can balance both.

— *Confused Husband*

DEAR HUSBAND: Not only women lose their sex drive; my own inbox reveals that men lose their drive too. You are incorrect when you assert that there are no medical reasons for this. Myriad physical and psychological issues come into play.

The way you portray your marriage — being with your best friend, getting along well and basically living peacefully — makes it sound ideal in many ways. There is a high likelihood that even if you found a new partner, the same sexual dynamic would settle in if you were lucky enough to be together for almost two decades. You are fortunate to have a happy relationship to build upon.

You don't mention speaking to your wife about this. You also don't mention things you could do differently to ignite the spark and keep the flame burning. Before you resort to making assumptions about people having affairs, you should try the universal aphrodisiac: communication. Intimacy starts there.

Therapy's utility is really up to the client

DEAR AMY: I have been with my partner for more than 10 years, and while it has always been a challenging relationship, I take seriously the idea of honoring the commitment I made to him.

He has many issues with his family and his parents, and says he cannot overcome these no matter how hard he tries. We have seen various therapists over the years, and our counselors have told him that he is not addressing the "big" topics.

When he comes home from therapy, I sometimes ask him what they discussed, and he'll say they talked about his job, his concerns about money or his minor physical maladies, but he never says that they have discussed big "breakthrough" topics or really tough stuff.

One of our joint therapists told me that she felt he was evading his biggest issues. I want to help him if I can (and urge him to keep trying therapy) but I find it very difficult to live in a home where big, difficult topics aren't addressed, where it doesn't feel as if there's any momentum — and I feel we're really drifting apart.

Is there any way I can help him to see that the problems won't just solve themselves, and that to move forward together, each one of us has to take the steps? We can't walk for each other.

— *Committed in California*

DEAR COMMITTED: Your approach to therapy is, "Go big or go home." Your guy wants to jawbone about his job, money and health. But guess what? It's his therapy. He gets to discuss whatever he wants, and he shouldn't have to do therapy in any particular way to please you.

Your own therapist should counsel you: "What if your guy never, ever faces these 'big' issues? What if he never masters therapy the way you have?"

You've said it best yourself: "We can't walk for each other." Don't walk for him. Concentrate on what you can do in your own life to either accept him as he is or make some changes on your own.

Silent treatment speaks volumes

DEAR AMY: My husband gives me the silent treatment on a regular basis, generally as a response to some innocuous action, like leaving a pencil on the table, or his dislike of my lunch friends at work. Our reconciliations occur only if I approach him and make peace. He never makes any attempt to reconcile, apologize or discuss.

I find this behavior very damaging to my confidence. I find myself resentful after these episodes if he wants to be affectionate because I never know how he will behave. He seems to prefer to pretend that these episodes never happened.

— *Tired of Peacemaking*

DEAR TIRED: Of course your husband would prefer to pretend that these episodes never happened. That's because his reaction to you is immature, rude and wrong, and he knows it.

I'm not sure what crime you might have committed by leaving a pencil on a table, but if this infraction brings on a period of punishing silence, your husband has a real problem. His reaction is controlling and unhealthy for both of you.

It is completely possible to change this dynamic, but first he must recognize that the key to a good marriage is robust communication, and that means he must learn to express himself respectfully. Ask your husband to join you in counseling. If he isn't willing to try to behave differently, you'll have a difficult choice to make about your marriage. This situation will not improve on its own.

TV, laptop make bedroom crowded

DEAR AMY: Increasingly, over the last year, my wife's work has gotten busier. As soon as we put our kids to bed, she begins working on her laptop, often past 1 a.m. She isn't thrilled about having to work, so she wants to do the work in "cozy" surroundings in our bed with the TV on.

The problem is that I am not a night owl and like to get seven hours of sleep, which is impossible when she is working in bed, furiously typing away on her laptop until the wee hours of the morning.

She keeps insisting that the work frenzy will soon pass, but I don't get the sense this will happen. Do you have any suggestions for finding some middle ground?

— *Sleepless in Portland*

DEAR SLEEPLESS: There are some obvious technical fixes to mitigate this problem: Your wife could use headphones, a quieter keyboard and a filter against the laptop's glow. However, none of those little remedies touches the real issue, which is that your bedroom should be a refuge from work and television. Especially with young children in your lives, you two need a place in your home where you can rest, recharge and be intimate. If you move the TV out of the room, you both will get more sleep.

I take it as a given that your wife is spending her nighttime hours working, rather than trolling Facebook. If so, she might be able to do her work during more reasonable hours, if you share your home chores efficiently.

Fiancé's character is more a question than finances

DEAR AMY: I recently became engaged to a wonderful man. He was raised in an affluent family and given every opportunity to be successful, which he is.

My background is very multicultural and working-class. As a couple, my fiancé and I enjoy deep conversations about the world. The problem is that his outlook on people is very different from mine. I think all humans have the innate ability to be successful with hard work, ambition and opportunity. My fiancé has a disregard for people he sees as being "inferior."

I have many family members who might be considered by him to be in this "inferior" class. I have a huge problem with this. He says that I am taking his comments out of context, and that he is referring to other people and not my family.

This is getting to be a deal-breaker. Can we work this out, or are we too different?

— *Worried*

DEAR WORRIED: Differences in culture, background and outlook need not be deal-breakers. In fact, differences can inspire people toward growth.

But this is more than a culture clash — this is a character clash. At the end of the day, does it really matter whether your fiancé is trashing your family specifically — or merely everyone else who doesn't make the grade?

It is possible to squelch or alter a superior attitude, but it's not really possible to change a person's DNA. You can't "work out" a person's character. Don't get married until you two dig in and explore his attitude — and your intolerance toward him — thoroughly with clergy and/or a couples counselor.

Phone affair damaging emotionally

DEAR AMY: My spouse developed a telephone addiction for a childhood friend. This relationship has been going on for several years but my husband has never mentioned it to me.

I learned of this by accident from a friend of the family. When I approached him he downplayed it as minimal casual contact. Later he admitted he had a special connection with her and said that they are in touch often. He also says they are "just friends" and refuses to cut ties with her and her family.

If they are "just friends" I cannot understand the total secrecy of this relationship (her husband was equally clueless). It is as if they had conducted an intimate physical affair. The emotional distress has been devastating to me psychologically and it has devastated our marriage.

I am made out to be the villain by my husband and the other woman for demanding an end to it. I have been a faithful wife and do not know how to deal with this.

What should I do?

— *Devastated Wife*

DEAR DEVASTATED: Judging from the contents of my inbox, emotional affairs are the new infidelity. I don't want to make it seem like these nonsexual affairs are some sort of fad-of-the-heart. They are very real, tangible and painful — as your story illustrates.

Marriage is like a house built by two people; the house's function is to contain the intimate relationship. Your husband has opened a window onto this other relationship without your knowledge or consent.

I borrow the "open window" metaphor from the important book on this subject, "Not 'Just Friends': Rebuilding Trust and Recovering Your Sanity After Infidelity," by Shirley P. Glass and Jean Coppock Staeheli (2004, Free Press). The authors' research on infidelity shows that for many people, emotional infidelity is actually far worse than a sexual affair.

You and your husband can mediate your way through this with the help of a marriage counselor. I agree that if he continues to maintain this secret and exclusive relationship it will seriously impair, if not destroy your marriage.

Marriage is not about independence, but interdependence

DEAR AMY: My wife and I are retired. We have not had a vacation in more than 10 years because we have quite a large sum tied up in our lovely home.

Several days ago she announced she was going on a two-week vacation with a female friend. There was no discussion before the decision was made. I asked how we would afford it. Her reply: "I'll put it on my credit card" and use our airline miles.

In the past I have never suggested she pay for any part of a vacation with her personal money. We paid for our trips out of what I call our family money (money I earned working or retirement funds).

We have been on many great vacations in the past, including Europe, Hawaii, etc. She believes that I'm selfish and controlling and feels at times I'm holding her back. She says she should be able to do what she wants. I feel she is the selfish one.

Please give me your opinion.

— Left Behind

DEAR LEFT: I agree with you. You and your wife are wrestling over control, and she is willing to selfishly plunge you both into debt in order to assert her independence. But marriage isn't necessarily about independence. It is about interdependence.

You should use this as your reason to mediate this and other issues with a counselor. You both need financial as well as marriage counseling.

Clock is ticking for him to propose

DEAR AMY: I am 39 years old, soon to be 40, and have been in an exclusive relationship with my boyfriend, whom I love very much, for a little over a year.

We met through mutual friends and had a friendship before we started dating, so we were fortunate to have a foundation a lot of other couples don't have. Neither of us has been married before, but it is something that both of us want. We also both want to have children.

I have been very upfront and open with him about wanting marriage and kids, in that order. I have also been upfront with him about my biological clock, which is ticking loud and fast.

Although we have had some very serious and in-depth conversations about our future, including marriage and kids, over the last six or so weeks — and he assures me I am the one, and he wants to marry me — he has yet to "pop the question."

He is a very careful and cautious person, more slow-moving than anyone I have been with before. However, I am feeling unsatisfied and frustrated with the relationship as it is and am ready for him to take it the next level. I have communicated to him clearly where I would like things to go.

Is it shortsighted of me to set a date in the future for him to commit to marriage or jump ship? I can't hang out in limbo much longer.

— *Worried*

DEAR WORRIED: You have been very upfront with your guy (and good for you). You need to realize and understand the pressure this imposes on him. You also need to realize that if you break up over this, any subsequent relationship will be under even more pressure.

Ideally, you two would continue to navigate this together. You could propose to him by saying, "I'd like to get married in the fall; what do you think of this idea?" Encourage him to be completely honest with you about this, with a promise of no hard feelings if he can't quite get there.

You (and he) may feel that it detracts from the "romance" of a proposal to do it this way, but there is nothing more romantic than making a mutual decision to march through life together. Ultimately, it doesn't matter who "pops the question."

Is this a 'civilized' or tawdry affair?

DEAR AMY: My wife left me. I still live near her family. Her family has taken my side because she left me, even though she and I have tried our best to avoid the blame game.

Her 19-year-old niece started helping me out when I had my young sons on the weekend. We started having sex. I didn't seduce her. It just happened. I tried to stop, but we didn't.

There's a 14-year age difference between us. My ex-wife figured out what was going on and called me. Instead of being angry, she teased me at first and then said she was happy that I was with her niece.

Maybe my ex and I are a little too civilized. We were never all that passionate about each other, which led to my ex finding someone else.

Her niece and I have been very passionate, but I wonder if it's the dark, taboo side that is the basis of the attraction. Now she wants to move in with me. When she told her mother, her mom took her to Victoria's Secret to celebrate.

I want an objective opinion. Are we nuts?

— *Worried*

DEAR WORRIED: There are children involved in your tawdry tale. Every choice you make should be for their benefit.

There is no such thing as being "too civilized," but you and your ex might be playing a mind game with each other. This family seems to be pushing the two of you together (the mother taking your young lover to Victoria's Secret to celebrate your relationship is icky).

You have the freedom to have a sexual relationship with anyone; what you mustn't do is involve the kids in what is potentially a very messy situation. When this relationship cools (and it will), you will face the prospect of alienating your kids' extended family.

Whatever you choose, do not cohabit. You should explore your ability to have a relationship without leaping (or being pressured) into a domestic commitment.

Turn back the clock to fix finances

DEAR AMY: I recently got remarried. My two sons are in college, and I have a full-time teaching job, a house that is almost paid off and a substantial nest egg. My husband is moving in with me soon but has debts from his business.

Before we were married (we were friends), I gave him $16,000 to help keep his business afloat. I don't expect repayment. He still has $25,000 in credit card debt accrued from his business at about a 12 percent interest rate, which he will still need to pay while he is looking for work when he moves to my state. I could sell some of my investments to pay off his credit card, but I am not sure if I should do that.

I know that it would make sense to pay off a high-interest bill, but I hesitate to sell investments to give him more money. What should I do?

— *Newlywed*

DEAR NEWLYWED: I think you should turn back the clock and have a series of important financial conversations and negotiations before you get married.

I'm going to get you started on your "postnup" conversation by suggesting questions: Who owns the home you two will share? Who is responsible for your sons' college tuition? Who is responsible for your husband's credit card debt? Are you willing to help finance a new business for him? If he gets a job, will you combine incomes? Who will handle household bills? Will you happily share your retirement savings?

A certified public accountant or financial planner can walk you through this without overwhelming you. Also, read "It's Not You, It's the Dishes: How to Minimize Conflict and Maximize Happiness in Your Relationship," by Paula Szuchman and Jenny Anderson (2012, Random House).

Engagement etiquette is up to the couple

DEAR AMY: I am hoping you can clarify proper etiquette for marriage proposals for all the men out there. I was having a conversation recently with a group of young men in their 30s, and there were many misconceptions about marriage proposals.

I'm worried that should these men ever propose, their girlfriends are going to be very disappointed. For example, two of the men thought it was acceptable to propose without a ring! I feel strongly that men should have a ring on hand when proposing. Am I just old-fashioned, or are these men oblivious?

— *Wondering*

DEAR WONDERING: I don't think this is really an etiquette question. Proposals are all about the couple embarking on their happy ever after, and there is no one way to do this.

Many couples consider ring shopping together to be part of the ritual of getting engaged. When I proposed to my husband, I forgot the ring part altogether — and fortunately he has forgiven me.

Family

. . . .

You Don't Choose Them, but Sometimes They Pick Up the Tab

Face fears, tell parents about sex life

DEAR AMY: My boyfriend and I have been in a loving relationship for a little over a year. We are both teenagers and above the age of consent in our state (I am 16). We are very much in love and incredibly happy. Recently we had a couple of serious conversations about sex, and we decided to go ahead and do it.

It was the first time for both of us and was very special. We were safe and responsible, and neither of us has any regrets. However, my parents do not know that we are sexually active, and they do not seem to trust me to be safe and responsible about my decisions.

I worry that if they found out the degree to which we are intimate, they would force us to break up. I would like to be able to talk to them about this, but I have no idea how to broach the subject, and frankly I'm scared of their reaction. Please tell me how I can talk to them and convince them that I am mature enough to handle this level of intimacy.

— *Anonymous in New England*

DEAR ANONYMOUS: According to the Guttmacher Institute, 7 of 10 American teens have had intercourse by age 19 and a sexually active teenager who doesn't use a contraceptive has a 90 percent chance of becoming pregnant within a year.

You should go to your physician or to Planned Parenthood for a checkup and STD and birth control counseling. If you and your guy are unable to face this task together, then you should not be in a sexual relationship. Check plannedparenthood.org or call 800-230-PLAN (7526) for a local clinic.

The reason your parents might not trust you is because they were your age once and they know how momentous this choice is — and how physically and emotionally vulnerable you both are. Your parents have the utmost stake in your emotional and physical health.

Your desire to talk to your folks about this tells me that you have a good relationship and simply want to be honest with them. Share this first with the parent you are closest to, but remember this: Your honesty will also inspire their honest reaction.

They may be very upset. But if they are thoughtful, they will appreciate the opportunity to talk it through with you. (Your boyfriend should also talk to his parents.) The Planned Parenthood website also has resources for parents.

Stepkids are 'real'; family must deal

DEAR AMY: When I married my wife, she had two kids and I had two kids. We became a very happy blended family of six and have been together for 12 years.

My wife's extended family has accepted this. They always include all four children for holidays and recognize all the kids' birthdays. They love all four kids equally, and it shows at family functions. You can just feel the love; it's very warm and welcoming.

My family has a problem and just can't accept our blended family. They exclude two of my children (my stepkids) on birthdays, graduations, Christmas, family functions, conversations, etc. It really hurts me to see my own family exclude my children.

My sister frequently tells my wife that her kids are not blood-related to us, and she rubs this in my wife's face a lot. The hurt in my wife's eyes is hard for me to handle. I married my wife and want to protect her from all of this. It's hard to accept that, with all the things in this world that could hurt my wife, it's my family that hurts her the most.

I'm so ashamed. How can I get my family to understand how hurtful their actions are?

— Sad Dad

DEAR SAD: You have had more than a decade to train your family to be decent people and let them adjust to reality, which roughly translates to this: "My wife and I have four children. Deal with it."

You have not advocated for your wife and children. Now, rather than passively commenting on how sad your wife's eyes are when she is disrespected in your presence, I suggest you act a little less sad and get a lot more mad.

The next time your sister expresses this level of disrespect toward your wife and children, your reaction should be consistent: "This is unacceptable. Get your coat; it's time to go."

You owe your wife and all of your children an apology. Say: "My family members are ignorant and have been very rude to all of us. We are 100 percent family, and I'm going to try to do a better job of being a dad to all of you."

When you tolerate this sort of disrespect, your stepchildren aren't the only ones affected. This treatment places your biological children in a terrible spot with their siblings. I'm sure it makes them uncomfortable, embarrassed and sad.

Grandparents feel slighted by teen

DEAR AMY: My son dated and subsequently married a divorced woman with a daughter, "Chelsea," who is now 13. When we became aware of this child in his life, we sent her $100 gifts for her birthday (late October) and for Christmas. We've done this for the past five years.

My son is the CPA for a famous band, so we get to see Chelsea each December when the band performs in our hometown.

We have never been thanked for these gifts. In fact, the girl totally ignored us at the concert this year, even though she was talking to her uncles not 3 feet away from us! The blatant lack of respect bothered me so much that I asked my son to address the problem with his wife, but he angrily told me not to give anymore gifts if I expected to get thanked. I raised my son to always thank a person for a gift. Usually, a card was sent.

I really love my daughter-in-law and don't want to cause any problems.

— *Disrespected*

DEAR DISRESPECTED: Try to see this from "Chelsea's" point of view. She is at a high-octane concert with other relatives when two people she barely knows stand not 3 feet away. She thinks these people are her stepdad's parents, but she only sees them once a year. And she doesn't know what to call them (is it "Mr. and Mrs. Martin"?), so she's not sure how to strike up a conversation. Oh, and she's 13, so every single situation makes her uncomfortable.

I agree with you that the parents should smooth things out here, but they're not doing their job and you're making things worse. You should stop focusing on your gifts and start trying to figure out how to get to know her. That way, when she sees you she will be able to greet you and pay you some much-needed attention.

Everyone must dance to dad's tune

DEAR AMY: For years my husband has been controlling which television programs we watch and which radio stations we listen to. When I choose a radio station, he tells me the music is garbage and will tune it to his station. Until now, I've never felt it was worth arguing over.

Yesterday he was out of the house, and I was listening to a station that my daughters and I enjoy. When my husband came home, my daughter expressed her concern that the station was "not one of daddy's." She didn't want to be confronted by him and went upstairs.

Sure enough, he came in, realized that it was not one of his stations, said the music was garbage and turned off the radio, despite my objections. He does the same thing with the television. His inflexibility and dominating behavior are obvious in other situations that are more important to me (such as the extreme lack of organization in the house and his unwillingness to look for a job).

He is a stay-at-home dad. This was great while the kids were little, but due to instability in my own professional position this is now causing concern.

— *Unable to Change Course*

DEAR UNABLE: You have wrapped many complaints about your husband into one bundle. From your account, he is intimidating and domineering, so intimidating that he has trained your daughter that he literally owns the airwaves. Imagine the impact of his behavior on your girls' impression of how men do/should behave.

This is not about a clash of media taste, though I believe that whoever occupies a room first (or is making dinner) gets to choose the playlist (truly tasteless or degrading music and commentary are not for public consumption and, like the Supreme Court, the adults declare that we know where the line is when we hear it). I agree that he needs to change in many ways for you to have a happier household. You should try to mediate some of these issues in couples counseling. Failing that, if you are unwilling to leave the marriage, you should pursue counseling to learn why you stay.

Tell kids truth about 'messy' family

DEAR AMY: My dad and I have a mostly estranged relationship. He was absent most of my life, and now we only communicate through an occasional text message. He is now married to wife No. 3, and up until a few months ago she seemed like a nice enough person — until he revealed that she had an affair and at 46 became pregnant with another man's baby.

My father and she separated but have now reconciled and have decided to raise this baby together (my dad is 63), along with the man she had the affair with. I told him I respected his personal decision. His wife recently asked to list me on Facebook as family, and I had such a negative reaction to it I blocked her completely. I only met her once years ago and have no personal connection to her.

I would like to visit my dad with my children. They have asked about him, and despite the lack of relationship, I still love him and would like him to know his grandchildren. However, I really don't want anything to do with her or this child. I don't want to have to explain the whole thing to my kids, adding to the already messy family dynamic.

I think this offended my dad, as he takes his marriage vows very seriously from a religious perspective. (He annulled the marriage from to my mother and made his current wife get two annulments before they could marry.)

Am I out of line to ask to see only him when I visit?

— *Daughter*

DEAR DAUGHTER: Your father can't take marriage vows all that seriously if he is on his third marriage, but regardless — he is embracing the existence of this child and is helping to raise it, which is the right thing to do, especially seeing as how the child's mother is his wife.

So you come from a messed-up family. Join the club.

You are responding to the confusion and complication by essentially trying to erase an entire person — a child who has done nothing to deserve being shunned or denied by you or anyone else. The child does have a biological father, and it also seems right for this man to have a hand in raising the child.

You should be truthful with your children, despite how painful or embarrassing this is for you. You can certainly ask to see your father alone, but don't be surprised if he doesn't agree to this condition.

Dad's next wedding feels freakishly familiar

DEAR AMY: My dad is getting remarried and I need advice. His wedding plans sound fun, and I know he means well, but this wedding sounds freakishly similar to his wedding with my mother.

My sister "Rachel" was 7 and I was an infant when our parents got married. I've seen their wedding pictures and heard stories about their big family party. Most of the relatives from the first wedding will be attending this wedding and after-wedding party, and I don't want word to get to his bride that he is re-creating his first wedding. Because of this peculiar situation, I am not sure of what to do.

— *Concerned Daughter*

DEAR CONCERNED: When you say these two weddings are "freakishly similar," are you saying that both weddings feature common elements such as your dad, extended family, clergy and a cake?

Or are you saying that both weddings are in the same location, with the same musicians, flowers and featuring a cake with your mother's name crossed out and your stepmother's name written underneath it?

Many weddings have similar elements, but if you and your sister feel this event is so like the earlier one that people will be whispering about it across the aisles, then you should speak up.

Tell your father, "Dad, I know I was a baby the last time around, but from pictures I've seen it looks like your upcoming wedding is going to be identical to the wedding you had with Mom. 'Rachel' and I are wondering if that's such a good idea."

Grandma frets over daughter's men

DEAR AMY: I am the grandmother of three beautiful children, ages 4, 6 and 10, whom I live with and help raise.

Their mother (my daughter) has been involved in approximately six relationships over the past three years, with a two-to-three-week interval between relationships. I am wondering if it is a good idea for her to have these men sleeping in her bed every night, visible to the kids, and also whether it is OK for them to sleep with her and the men.

I am looking for an objective answer.

— *Grandmother*

DEAR GRANDMOTHER: It is not good for the children to have six different men in their lives and living in the home with them. I also think it is a terrible idea to have children sleeping alongside two adults who I presume are sexually active. Having men unrelated to the children passing through the home places them at risk. This is also emotionally confusing.

You are also living in the home. I assume you have raised this issue and that your daughter either does not agree with your opinion or does not care what you think. You are essentially co-parenting the children with your daughter but have no say in a very basic issue such as who lives in the house with you. Nor do the children have a say in the matter.

You and your daughter could benefit from attending parenting classes together. That way you could both receive objective in-person opinions (and perhaps mediation) on what is best for the children. However, this is a matter of common sense; your daughter either doesn't possess this very basic judgment or is simply too selfish to care. I hope you can continue to advocate for the children.

Mother's things need new home

DEAR AMY: My nephew's mother died when he was 15. When my brother passed away a few years later, we were the only blood relatives he had left, although his girlfriend's family became a surrogate family for him. They have done everything possible to alienate the family, and it seems to have worked.

My nephew is now 24. He will not come to any family gatherings, ignores e-mails, text messages, phone calls, etc., and lies to people about how the family has cut him off.

He married his girlfriend recently, and that was the last contact any of us has had with him. It's painful, but I've decided that I can't force him to stay in touch. I need to move on with my life.

I have his mother's expensive jewelry and want to give it to him. He refuses to meet with me to receive it. I considered mailing it to him, but he won't tell me where he lives. Should I give up and wait for him to contact me?

— *Feeling Guilty*

DEAR GUILTY: You should write a letter to your nephew's in-laws (the people you say became his "surrogate" family). Even though they have alienated your nephew from you, you should attempt to fulfill your duty to give his mother's property to him.

In the letter, say that you miss him and regret this loss. Ask them to have him contact you regarding this property.

Tension over gratitude crosses generations

DEAR AMY: Frequently, grandparents who write to you complaining that their grandchildren do not write thank you notes. Do they write thank you notes to their grandchildren?

My children spend time before each birthday, Mother's Day, Father's Day and Christmas choosing things they think their grandparents will like. Not once have my children received a thank you note for a gift they have given to their grandparents.

While I believe a verbal thank-you when a gift is received on some occasions is enough, my children's grandparents want a written note for every gift. My children dutifully write the notes but frequently ask why their grandparents never write notes thanking them for the gifts they choose.

— *Tired of the Double Standard*

DEAR TIRED: I completely agree with you that your kids' grandparents are not only demanding and unreasonable about this, but they are also modeling the kind of ingratitude they decry.

I suggest you have a heart-to-heart with them, remind them of their standards and ask them to mind their manners.

Family is worried for bullied child

DEAR AMY: My beautiful 11-year-old niece is being bullied at school. She is petite, so other children make fun of her size. She has learned to ignore this, but yesterday this teasing escalated to the point where a fellow student told her she was going to be beaten up.

My niece has talked to the teachers and school counselor, but now she has the reputation of being a snitch, so she doesn't want to take that route again.

Things are so bad for her that she gets knots in her stomach and a headache every school day and doesn't want to go back to school. Her parents, my husband and I are at a loss as to what to tell her. Do you have any suggestions on how we can help her?

— *Worried Aunt*

DEAR AUNT: Your niece's parents should be all over this issue with the school. The child who made this threat should be dealt with (and the child's parents should be called in).

Your niece did the right thing by taking this to adults at school, and now the other adults in her life should rally behind and beside her to assure her that you are on her side as you help her to tackle this.

You and her parents can encourage your niece to get involved in activities to build and bolster her self-esteem. Dance, gymnastics, swimming and other sports can help her to feel strong despite her size. These activities also will introduce her to other kids outside of the classroom. Academic teams, Scouting, music and theater will help her to be more confident.

You can also help her by telling stories from your own life. You can ask her to describe her feelings and review strategies for dealing with them. Friendship is an ideal antidote to bullying. Help to foster friendships at and outside of school.

Daughter, stepdad splitting over religion

DEAR AMY: I am a 16-year-old girl, and I live with my mom and step-father. My stepfather has been in my life since I was 10, and we've always gotten along very well. Lately, though, we have been clashing.

My mom and my stepdad switched churches to better suit their spiritual needs a couple of years ago, while I kept the religion that my mom raised me with. They don't talk about their religion, and I hardly ever talk about mine unless somebody else brings it up.

More than once, my stepdad has asked me a question about my religion, I have answered it, and he has argued with me about it. These arguments do not pertain to his, only mine. The arguments usually end with me walking away fuming.

I don't confront him about his religion because I fear he will get upset, as I do when he confronts me about mine. I don't talk to him about these arguments because I fear it would only ignite another argument.

What should I do? I want to have a good relationship with my stepdad. Am I right to be so annoyed when he lectures me about my religion?

— Annoyed With Arguments

DEAR ANNOYED: There is nothing right or wrong about being annoyed. What counts is what you do about your feelings and how you choose to express them.

It is legitimate to want to steer clear from these conversations to preserve your good relationship with your stepfather. I think it's a wise instinct on your part. You should try to talk to him, not about your respective religions but about your conversations. You could say to him, "I feel that whenever we discuss this I end up getting upset.

That's why I don't bring it up. Maybe we should just agree not to talk about it."

Your mother might be able to explain what's behind these arguments. Your folks might be upset that you didn't choose to switch religions along with them.

Long-ago allegation of violence haunts daughter

DEAR AMY: My parents divorced after five years of marriage when I was 3. My father remained an active part of my life, and our relationship has always been good.

When I was in elementary school, my mother told me that she had divorced my father because he was physically abusive. From time to time, she would tell me the details of his violent outbursts.

I am now 42 and simply cannot believe he would have raised his hand in anger to my mother or anyone else (he has been happily married for 31 years to my stepmother). My mother exaggerates, sometimes wildly, and now I wonder if these allegations are true. I asked her siblings about this, and they had no knowledge of any violence in the marriage.

I have a nagging desire to ask my father about this. I feel he should have the opportunity to clear his name. I also want to find out if my mother lied. So, should I ask?

— *To Ask or Not To Ask*

DEAR ASK: By all means, ask. But realize that this might not be a satisfying experience for either of you.

Say, "Dad, I love you. I know you and Mom weren't married for very long, but Mom told me you had been violent toward her. I love you regardless of anything that might have happened so long ago, but this is weighing on my mind. Can you tell me if this is true?"

This is a dangerous and damaging allegation; I can understand why you would want to try to learn the truth.

Stepdaughter devastated at loss of opportunity

DEAR AMY: My mother died after 14 years of marriage to her husband, my stepfather. That was two years ago. During that time the blended family was encouraged to think of ourselves as a family and not as "steps." This man was the only grandfather my children (now young adults) have ever known.

Now my stepfather is remarrying. My immediate family has not been included in the engagement or wedding notices or plans; we are not invited to the wedding. I'm feeling a bit deserted by this. Am I overreacting?

— Left Out

DEAR LEFT OUT: Your reaction is natural and understandable. If you feel you still have a wonderful and warm relationship with your stepfather and are baffled by this exclusion, you might assume that it is due to sensitivity on the part of your stepfather's fiancé.

She may be uncomfortable with or feel threatened by the relationship your stepfather has with you. This is unfortunate. You should tell your stepfather that you are happy for him and that you and the kids miss him very much.

You could invite her to meet you for lunch or a drink. This might ease the way toward a new blending of your family.

This year, forgiveness is best gift

DEAR AMY: I have four grandchildren: two adolescents who live out of town and two toddlers close to home. I have always been generous with all of them at birthdays and Christmas.

My "out-of-town" 16-year-old grandson treated us rudely when we visited recently (we don't see them very often). On a previous visit to our home, he was destructive and we had to replace some items. We talked to his father (our son) about it, and he said he would make the boy pay for his damage. Of course that never happened.

The parents are divorced and seem to have a "communication" problem. I know he is angry at his dad, but he should know not to take that out on everyone else.

I want to know how to let him realize that I am not to be taken advantage of! You can't be disrespectful and expect me to reward you with gifts. I don't want to be mean, but I will no longer be made a fool of. If I send gifts to his sister on Christmas, I can't ignore him — but how can I send this message to him without appearing spiteful and vengeful? His mother is no help.

— *Upset Grandmother*

DEAR GRANDMOTHER: You claim that a 16-year-old should know how to express his anger and confusion appropriately. But how will he know this if the adults in his life don't lead the way? (His parents don't sound like the best examples to follow.)

Teenagers flail about, acting out their feelings and frustrations, and it is the adults in their lives who should show them the way by being consistent, patient and forgiving. From your account, this boy has had his share of challenges. Can you imagine that maybe he was testing you? And have you passed this test?

Firmness is called for, of course, but you don't seem to have expressed your concerns and consequences to him directly or maturely. I'd like to ask you to consider an alternative.

Forgive him for Christmas. Love him as much as you can — even in his currently messy state and even when he acts unlovable — and use this as an opportunity to let him experience how beautiful it feels to be forgiven, even when everybody knows he has messed up badly.

Include long-established partners in family events

DEAR AMY: My son is 24 and has been dating the same girl for seven years. Should I be inviting her to bridal/baby showers for my family? I thought I was just letting her off the hook, but maybe it's an insult? She's not very social or verbal with us, but maybe this would help.

— *Mom*

DEAR MOM: Do the math. This is an excellent example of familial geometry. Seven years of being "let off the hook" might feel to her like seven years of being excluded. You say this young woman isn't very social, but then you aren't, either.

A longtime girlfriend should be enfolded in your family. If you do this now and she becomes an "official" member of your family, she'll know the ropes.

Should teen be bathing with kids?

DEAR AMY: What is your thinking about an 18-year-old aunt taking a bath with her nephews — one boy almost 2, the other almost 3? If the genders were reversed and the 18-year-old was a male and the children were females, the teenager would probably be arrested.

This concerned old granny would like your opinion. I will respect it.
— *A Concerned Granny*

DEAR GRANNY: I think this is completely unacceptable.

In addition to the sexual overtones, there are safety concerns here. An adult should supervise every second that these young children are in the tub — and not from inside the tub, but from the edge of the tub, where the adult can see and swoop in for the rescue, if necessary.

You don't go into detail about this family, but the red flags are flying high over this and as the responsible and concerned adult, you should act immediately to put a stop to it. These young children are at risk.

If you aren't able to intervene successfully to mentor the parent or parents involved to be more responsible and if you continue to be concerned about their welfare, you can call your local office of Child Protective Services and discuss your concern anonymously.

College choice is kid's conundrum

DEAR AMY: I am a junior in high school and am starting to think about what career I want to pursue and what universities I'd like to attend.

My parents hold jobs in the medical and criminal law fields, and my older sister is following in their footsteps. Three generations of my family have attended a prestigious university (my sister goes there now). Already, there is enormous pressure on me to go to this school and pursue a career in the sciences.

However, I want to study creative writing and journalism at an arts school. My immediate family has expressed disdain for this plan. They are convinced that though writing is a good "pastime," it is not a serious career choice. I resent having my career choices labeled as hobbies.

They say they will support whatever decision I make, but it doesn't feel like that. Should I follow them — or re-evaluate?

— *Help Wanted*

DEAR WANTED: Studying science does not preclude studying the arts. In fact, each field supplements and enhances the other.

One of my favorite writers, Abraham Verghese, is a physician who teaches at Stanford University's medical school and also holds a master of fine arts degree in writing from the University of Iowa.

If you have any interest in or aptitude for science, you could combine writing and science and have a great career. Go to the school that will offer you the most well-rounded education (this might be the "prestige" school). You can decide to specialize (or branch out) later.

Boyfriend's dirty-dancing past makes family nervous

DEAR AMY: My boyfriend and I have been together for five years and for all intents and purposes are a family, along with my teen daughters and his preschooler.

The other day we drove by an "adult dance club" and my boyfriend turned to my girls (ages 12 and 16) and told them that while he was in college he used to work there as a dancer. They replied with an uncomfortable and confused laugh and I quickly changed the subject.

I do not judge my guy for this past part-time job but I don't think it was appropriate for him to share this information with my daughters without checking with me first. I told him later that I felt it was inappropriate and confusing information to share with them. I feel he needs to respect my wishes not to bring this up again. He thinks I am overreacting. What do you think?

— *Unnecessary Information*

DEAR UNNECESSARY: For the sake of clarity, I'm going to assume that your guy was a male stripper. Now that I've made this assumption, let's conjure up a mental image and just go with it.

He is not ashamed of his past, and that might well be a good thing, but it is your right to expect family members to run important, confusing or fascinating personal factoids past you before disclosing them to the kids.

Now that he has told them, if they inquire you should be honest about it — including the fact that even though he did this before you met, it still makes you uncomfortable.

Dad pushes college student to meet his lady love

DEAR AMY: My parents' relationship always has been strained. About a year ago my father left home and moved to a different state. Surprisingly, he opened up about it and told me that he was living with another woman. I appreciate his honesty, but I have never met this woman nor do I particularly want to. Whenever he talks of living with her, it is uncomfortable, to say the least.

Recently he has been pushing me to come out and stay with them and meet his new partner because I'm headed to college in the fall. He even has had his new woman call me and ask me to come visit.

She seems nice, but I do not want to visit them — nor do I want to meet her. My father and I aren't close, but I tolerate him and have given him the benefit of the doubt numerous times.

Am I being immature? Should I tell him that I have no interest in meeting her, or is that rude?

— *Confused and College-bound*

DEAR CONFUSED: Your father is being honest with you. Treat him the same way. It's OK to say, "Dad, this makes me uncomfortable, and I'm just not ready."

A meeting will take away some of the uncertainty surrounding this, but your father should offer to bring her to visit with you, rather than trap you for a visit in their home before you are ready.

Relative's will makes husband burning mad

DEAR AMY: My husband is very angry that he was not included in a relative's will. He has spoken to a lawyer and is thinking about fighting it.

I am afraid this is going to start family problems and wish he would just forget about it. It is not a lot of money, but he feels it is not fair that he was not left anything.

He has been offered some furniture from the family, but he feels it is of less value than the money. Should I support his decision to take the family to court or continue to encourage him to take the property and move on?

— *Wife*

DEAR WIFE: Your husband's money might be better spent not on a lawyer but a therapist. Even if he managed to receive some money from the estate (which is doubtful), taking his family to court will shred these relationships.

It is anyone's right to cut someone out of a will. If your husband is going to blame someone for this situation, he should blame the person who drew up the will — not the beneficiaries.

You should urge your husband to accept this furniture and burn it or sell it if it would make him feel better. Then he should move on.

Ex returned to recharge, won't leave

DEAR AMY: I have been divorced from my son's father for more than 20 years. Our 22-year-old son lives with me. He agreed to stay home for a while after my second husband, of 15 years, died of a long illness. My son was a rock during this time.

My ex-husband needed a place to stay on a temporary basis until he could get his sales career profitable again, and I agreed to let him move in with us.

He had, over the past several years, made a poor and morally unpleasant decision to be involved in an illegal business operation, which was a failure on all fronts. He's sincerely trying very hard to get along with us, though it is not easy all around.

Five months later, he still can't afford his own place, and I'm totally sick of his company. Now my son has graduated from college and is actively searching for a professional job.

In three months, he wants to move out and live with a buddy. I fully support him in taking this step. Is it fair to set a boundary for my ex that he must leave when our son does?

My son is feeling bad, thinking he'll be kicking his dad to the curb just because he wants to move on with his own life. I worry that he will take a pass on his own opportunities out of guilt.

We're in a tough spot while trying to help a guy make a change in his life. What do you suggest?

— In a Pickle

DEAR PICKLE: You should not link your son's choices to his father's. He probably feels as conflicted as you do, but the sooner he faces the reality of his father's limitations, the better he will be able to draw his own boundaries.

You provided emergency housing for your ex. Surely he can continue to make professional progress from another address. You could help him find an inexpensive room to rent in a private home and give him a month to get there.

Explain to your son that his own job at this point of his life is to move on and move out. He has proved himself to be a wonderful family member, but he cannot be responsible for his parents' choices.

Child's bedwetting exposes parental issues

DEAR AMY: My daughter told me recently that she and her husband have been taking turns getting up during the night to wake up their 8-year-old son, "Ben." She said he has been sleeping so deeply that he won't wake up to use the bathroom.

I'm very concerned. I believe the bed-wetting could be caused by any number of things. This could be a medical issue, bullying at school or sexual abuse.

My daughter and her husband struggle to make their marriage work. Neither one wants to get help, and they say they're too busy for counseling. Now I'm afraid that their son may be in danger of having his problems ignored.

I struggled through childhood as a bed-wetter who was being sexually abused, and having no one address the problem resulted in years of chaos.

I love her and my grandkids. How can I encourage her to deal with this issue without alienating her?

— *Concerned Mom*

DEAR MOM: Bed-wetting is fairly common at this age. You might be overly alarmed because of your own history, but I agree with you that the parents should be willing to explore all of the possible causes and work with the boy to remedy them.

The most you can do is what no one did for you — be on the child's side without projecting your own history and anxiety onto him. Your daughter will eventually see that ignoring problems does not make them go away, but you can't force her to realize this.

For some people, advocating for your child brings the realization that you should advocate more for yourself. I hope she sees the connection.

Gay teen needs plan for coming out

DEAR AMY: I'm a 13-year-old boy, and I'm gay. I was wondering what advice you could give me on coming out to my parents. I don't know what to do or how to do it.

— *Lost*

DEAR LOST: It is a triumph to really know who you are, and you deserve credit for wanting to be your authentic and true self and to share this with your parents and others.

I shared your letter with Michael LaSala, who is a psychotherapist, professor at Rutgers University and author of the book "Coming Out, Coming Home: Helping Families Adjust to a Gay or Lesbian Child" (2010, Columbia University Press). LaSala is also gay and works with young people who are facing this challenge.

We both want to offer you our warmest support. Coming out is a process and you should prepare yourself as well as you can. LaSala suggests pondering some important questions:

"What are you hoping for in coming out to your folks?"

"What is the most realistic or likely outcome, and are you prepared for it? If your parents are part of a gay-intolerant religious or cultural tradition, or if you've heard them talk negatively about gay people, that tells you that even though they love you, they will have a tough time with this."

"Will they ask you to leave the house? You need to think about this possibility. Do you have a place to stay? Do you have a network of friends, family members, teachers and other adults you can turn to for emotional support?"

This is an adjustment for everyone, and even if your parents accept and enfold you (as we hope they will), you (and they) should be equipped with resources.

Look up these websites, and do some research (you can then share them with your parents): Parents, Families and Friends of Lesbians and Gays: pflag.org. Gay, Lesbian & Straight Education Network: glsen.org. The Trevor Project: trevorproject.org. (The Trevor Project runs a hotline staffed with counselors. Keep this number on hand: 866-488-7386.)

You should start this conversation by choosing a time, sitting down with your parents and saying, "Mom and Dad, I have something important to talk about."

Boundaries can promote balance

DEAR AMY: I am a young professional, and I am having a difficult time balancing my long-term romantic relationship and the close re-lationship I have with my family. Both relationships demand a lot of time, and planning a weekend gives me a headache because everyone feels entitled to my time!

I try to arrange my weekends so no one feels excluded, but I ulti-mately feel guilty no matter what I do. At least one of these relation-ships will certainly suffer (if it hasn't already). How should I handle this without really hurting someone?

— *Weekend Woes*

DEAR WOES: This issue will revisit you throughout your life, especially if you choose to have children, creating more relationships that you must manage. The primary relationship is the one you have with yourself, and until you value your lifelong friendship with yours truly, you will never be able to balance the ancillary relationships in your life.

So put yourself first. You will have to train yourself to value your own time, and then you'll have to retrain everyone in your life to respect your choices.

You will need to learn to say a firm, friendly and confident "no, thank you" to time demands that you can't (or don't want to) fulfill. If you are respectful and consistent, you won't be hurting anyone; if you continue to turn yourself inside out to please and accommodate everyone else in your life, you will hurt yourself.

Clergy may have been passed over for nuptial duty

DEAR AMY: My niece and her fiancé will be getting married soon. They asked me to officiate at the ceremony, and I agreed. Another relative just told me that the couple have since asked someone else to officiate. The couple have not mentioned any change in plans to me.

Meanwhile, I went to considerable trouble and expense to secure credentials required by state law to conduct the ceremony. What, if anything, should I say to the couple?

— *Dissed*

DEAR DISSED: First, you must find out if you're going to be strapping on your mail-order clerical collar for this wedding. So ask the couple, "Am I still on tap to officiate at your wedding? I'm all official and certified, so before I do any more preparation let me know what your final plans are."

Accept their answer with equanimity. Marrying couples frequently vacillate between choices until they figure out that the figurative left hand and right hand need to work together — in wedding planning and in life. You could consider this effort and expense your wedding gift to the couple.

Relatives want a return on graduation gift

DEAR AMY: My husband's nephew graduated from high school last June. His parents hosted a graduation party in his honor at their home. We gave him a substantial cash gift.

We have learned that he didn't graduate. Not only did he not graduate, but he and his family knew before the party that he was not graduating (he has left school and doesn't seem likely to ever graduate).

My husband wants the money back. I say it's too late and there's nothing he can do. He wants to talk to the nephew and his brother to get the money back. What do you think?

— *Miffed Relatives*

DEAR MIFFED: I agree that this family has behaved in a way that requires a response, but your husband's choice to demand his money back is unkind — and will not necessarily convey to his nephew the larger lesson.

Mainly, if he demands his money back, his brother and nephew will brand him a jerk and let themselves off the hook. And so while I disagree with your husband's choice, I also disagree with your assessment that there is nothing he can do.

He should contact both his brother and his nephew and express his confusion and disappointment over this family's deception.

He can say, "I don't get it. I'm really surprised that you would let people believe there was a graduation to celebrate when that simply wasn't the case. I'm also shocked that you would accept graduation gifts under these circumstances."

The brother and nephew should then offer to return the money (they probably won't do this, but it would be good to give them the opportunity to). It's possible (perhaps likely) that this family planned the party and then learned after the invitations had gone out that the boy wouldn't graduate. They maintained their plans to avoid embarrassment.

It seems that didn't work out so well.

Dad's computer history reveals porn

DEAR AMY: I share a home computer with my father.

Unfortunately, the computer history shows everything that happens within a week, and it shows that my dad has been looking at pornography.

My parents are divorced, and I realize he might be lonely, but I don't know how to approach it or if I even should. My dad and I are close, and I don't want the awkwardness of this to ruin our relationship. Should I ignore this and live with the awkwardness, or confront him and possibly ruin our relationship?

— *Awkward*

DEAR AWKWARD: Ignoring a situation is always the easiest thing to do in the short-term, but it seldom works long-term because family issues don't just go away.

Your father has a right to his own habits, however odious, as long as they aren't illegal or harming him or someone else. (I believe porn is harmful to all parties, but consenting adults have the right to make depressing choices.)

If you don't want to discuss this outright with your father (and who would?), you can split the difference by simply telling him, "Dad, the history of any previous searches shows up on our computer. If you don't want me to see what websites you've visited, you should clear out the history every day."

The awkwardness will subside, but if it doesn't and if you are concerned about your father (for this or any other reason), you should respectfully and forthrightly share your concerns.

Parenting

· ·

The Hardest Job You'll Ever Love

Youthful journals are cringe-worthy

DEAR AMY: I am in my late 30s, married with two children. I have many journals that I kept through my teens and 20s. I am wondering if I should keep these journals or dispose of them.

While my past is not terribly sordid or exciting, I know my husband would probably be hurt reading about past relationships (should he outlive me and find these diaries). My children would probably not be thrilled to read their mother's intimate thoughts and feelings from that era.

On one hand, I went through the trouble to write those journals, so I feel reluctant to get rid of them. If nothing else, they remind me of how far I have come in terms of my maturity and confidence. On the other hand, I cringe at the thought of others reading them, even after my death.

— *Not Anne Frank*

DEAR NOT: You need to define "cringe."

By cringe, do you mean, "I can't believe I spent so much time trying to mousse my hair like Rachel from 'Friends' "? Or do you mean, "I really wish I hadn't recorded my romantic obsession with my high school guidance counselor"?

I vote for keeping these diaries. Your intimate thoughts and feelings from another era are exactly what most children would be thrilled to read after their mother was gone, unless, of course, these contained untruths or cruel statements about family members.

If you want to redact passages which are particularly hurtful or cringe-worthy, this might be a good editorial exercise. (If you excise portions of your dairies and retype them, make sure to note the provenance of the content and the dates.) It might be fun to do this and also include "period" photos along with the text. Print out anything you retype and also keep an electronic version.

I'd enjoy running feedback from readers.

Daughter acts out, parents act worried

DEAR AMY: My 20-year-old daughter "Katie" has had her share of ups and downs with me and her dad. She has shown incredibly bad judgment by engaging in risky behavior, displays hypersexual tendencies and shows no remorse for the pain she has caused us over the years. She has struggled with manic depression since she was a teenager but will not take her medication or participate in therapy.

I have recently discovered that she is having an affair with a married teacher at the local high school. She is not even a little bit guilty about this. I saw one of their text messages, and it was like reading a chapter of "Fifty Shades of Grey." Now his wife has found out, so they are no longer hiding the affair. Katie refuses to discuss it with me. She will yell, slam doors and carry on if you try to approach any subject she does not want to discuss.

She is engaged to a nice guy. I really want to tell her fiancé about what is going on, but I don't know if I should. I have hinted to him that my daughter is not the "perfect angel" he has imagined her to be, but he refuses to listen.

I cannot even stand to be in the same room with my daughter knowing that she is lying to everyone by not coming clean about the nature of her relationship with this man. I keep wondering if I should contact the school to let them know what kind of teacher they are employing.

— *Disgusted and Confused*

DEAR DISGUSTED: Your daughter's behavior is distressing. I know it's a challenge to avoid being drawn in, but you should do your very best to distance yourself from her drama and to keep your focus on urging her to get treatment and protecting yourself from her emotional maelstrom. Focus on your own behavior — staying strong, calm and consistent.

I don't believe you should plow along, making phone calls and warning people about your daughter; you should seek professional support and advice for yourself about how to cope with (and react) to her. Author Kay Redfield Jamison offers professional and personal insight into bipolar disorder in her memoir, "An Unquiet Mind: A Memoir of Moods and Madness" (1997, Vintage). I highly recommend it.

Teen wants to go on ski trip; parents disagree

DEAR AMY: I'm a 15-year-old girl, and I have an excellent boy friend (not a boyfriend, but a friend who is a boy). He is 17 and wants to take me skiing one weekend.

We have been friends for a very long time, and I know him well. However, I am nervous that when I propose this short trip to my parents, they will be afraid that I will be attacked or something if I go with him alone. (We would be alone on this trip.)

Even though my parents don't know him, I trust him completely. Even if he tried something, I am a black belt in tae kwon do and would be able to defend myself. I really want to go on this trip, but my parents most likely won't consent. How can I prove to them that I am responsible and that they can trust a person who I trust?

— *Stressed for Trust*

DEAR STRESSED: Most parents wouldn't let their teen go away on a weekend trip alone with another teen (no matter the gender).

You are kidding yourself if you think a black belt in anything will serve to protect you in a vulnerable situation. In my view, running away might be the smartest defense if you are in trouble. But that's beside the point. You will win your parents' trust by being trustworthy. That means introducing them to your friends — especially this friend — and permitting them to do their job, which is to make decisions based on their (not your) best judgment.

Stepson squanders his financial aid

DEAR AMY: I have a 22-year-old stepson who is immature and irresponsible. He has been attending classes at a community college for four years and has yet to earn a degree! He spent some of his financial aid money last year to buy his girlfriend an engagement ring. (His fiancée's mother has now let him move into her home.) He needed $500 worth of repairs for his car, and instead of fixing it he went out and bought a $3,000 car with financial aid money. That car broke down in a week.

He took out a student loan for $8,000 because he needed money to pay off his credit cards. After all this, he borrowed $600 from his grandma for school supplies and she called my husband saying she needed her $600 back, so my husband paid her back, but did not require his son to repay us!

What should we do? My husband states we should do nothing because his son is grown and can make his own decisions. He says he has talked with his son and he won't listen, so he has to suffer the consequences of his decisions and actions.

I think he needs some tough love and I have told my husband that the only times his son should be given money from us is for his birthday.

— *Shaking My Head*

DEAR SHAKING: Your husband talks a good game, indicating that he knows what to do but is simply not ready or willing to do it.

You should work as a team to influence your stepson — and protect yourselves from his poor choices. Urge him to get a job. (If he values his education, he can attend classes at night.) You should never give him money. Nor should your husband repay money the son has "borrowed." The reason your husband should not leap in to repay debts and repair relationships is because when he does this he is preparing the "mark" for the next loan.

Your stepson may be committing fraud by using government-approved loans or financial aid for purposes other than his education. At the very least, his financial decisions are terrible. He needs financial counseling from a professional (not a parent). You and your husband cannot prevent others from enabling this young man. But if his father loves this young man, he will help him to find work, not another infusion of cash.

Treatment required for compulsive behavior

DEAR AMY: My daughter, 38, has been a compulsive skin picker since her teens. Her face and upper back bear the scars of this obsession.

Unfortunately, I did not realize when she was young that this is a form of OCD, responsive to a combination of counseling and medication. Instead, I simply implored her to "stop picking."

My daughter is a successful professional with a husband and two darling boys, but the habit persists. She often has scabs on her face.

I have offered to pay for counseling and have politely been told to back off.

I have promised not to bring it up again. Is there anything I can do? Send her literature on the subject? Show her your advice from this column?

— *Concerned Mother*

DEAR CONCERNED: At 38, your daughter is old enough to make choices about how she wants to handle her problems. She may take your offer to pay for counseling as being condescending.

If you have pointed out the possibility that she may have OCD; if you have told her that this condition often responds well to treatment; and if you have urged her to get help, then you have done what you should do. Respect her wishes and back off.

Mean girls might have mean moms

DEAR AMY: My 13-year-old daughter has been friends with three neighborhood girls since kindergarten, and I have been friends with their moms. In the past nine months, these girls have taken to "mean girl" behavior, and my daughter has been the target.

My daughter is resilient and has joined other groups at school. I never wanted to interfere, and I let my daughter work things out with these girls. One girl has since apologized and admitted she was being mean for no reason.

I sent Christmas cards to these families this year and expected cards in return, as has been the norm. None of these girls' families sent us a card this year.

I don't know what to do about this. Is it better to call these women and say, "Hey, I'm shocked and sorry your daughter is being mean to my daughter, but I wish we could work it out"? "I hope it doesn't damage our friendship"? Or should I ignore everything?

— *Confused Mom*

DEAR CONFUSED: If these women are normally in touch with you and have now, as a group, dropped you, then you can see where their daughters learned how to behave. You should approach this with the same honesty and resilience your own daughter has displayed.

If you want to try to revive these relationships, you could call these women individually to catch up. Based on their attitude toward you, you could then decide whether you want to maintain friendships.

You've done a good job of letting your daughter handle her own social challenges, and, unless these mean girls present an ongoing problem to her, you should leave the kids out of it.

Different last names creates mother/daughter confusion

DEAR AMY: I am a single mom with a 9-year-old daughter, "Sally." Her father and I never married, but he is very involved in her life. When Sally was born, we decided that she would have his last name, so I have a different last name than my daughter. I know this is not totally unusual, but it is obviously not the norm.

Evidently, many people on my side of the family have no idea that Sally has her father's last name, and it becomes apparent each year around the holidays. This past Christmas we received many holiday cards. Some people would address the cards to me and my daughter as "Kathy Smith and Sally," because they were unsure of her last name. But the majority of cards we got from my side of the family would address them as "Kathy and Sally Smith," even though Smith is not Sally's last name.

As my daughter gets older, it is starting to bother her more each time she sees it. I know this may seem like a trivial issue but is there some polite way I can let my family members know that Sally has a different last name than me? I love my extended family and don't want to insult them in any way.

— *Sally's Mom*

DEAR MOM: It is not insulting to be respectfully corrected.

Contact those family members who don't use "Sally's" last name and tell them, "I know it might seem confusing but Sally's last name isn't 'Smith,' its 'Jones'. She loves her last name, and it would be great if you could remember to use it when you're addressing envelopes."

You can prompt correct usage by having address labels and inexpensive stationary made for you and your daughter to use. This way any correspondence from either of you will come from "The Smith and Jones Family."

Otherwise, I hope you don't make too big a deal of this with your daughter. Tell her (as I told my daughter when she was young), "This is confusing for some people. So don't take it personally. It's like the old saying goes: 'I don't care what you call me — just don't call me late for dinner,' right?"

College choice reveals relationship flaw

DEAR AMY: My 17-year-old son, "Michael," lives with his mother in another city. He has been dating his girlfriend, "Emily," for two years. She is a smart, nice girl and generally a good influence on him. They are very close and spend all of their free time together.

I have talked to Michael about this, and Emily's mother has spoken to her, but we have not made any headway. I am concerned that my son does not have any friends outside of this relationship. Now the two of them are dead set on going to the same college. Emily has chosen a school, and Michael feels obliged to go there too, even though that may not be the best choice for him.

My son is a very high achiever and has a lot of options. While Emily's choice is a good school, I am against sending him to the same college for fear that he will miss the opportunity to grow as a person outside of this relationship. I'm also concerned that if they break up, he will be stuck in a school that isn't great for him with few or no friends other than her.

On the other hand, I don't feel as if I can just tell him where to go. My parents did that to me, and I resented it. I would gladly send him to a more expensive school, if it were a different school from Emily's.

— *Concerned Dad*

DEAR DAD: If "Emily" is isolating your son from his other friends and if the relationship is severely limiting his choices, he may be locked into a relationship that is not only exclusive, but abusive. There may be no reason to be alarmed, but you and the other adults should talk about it.

Part of your son's education is that he will be faced with the consequences of following someone to college, rather than leading himself there. If he is a high achiever, he will continue to be, and if he and his girlfriend break up, he will not be stuck at this school because he can exercise his options to stay or to transfer.

The real question is not about college but about why your son is in a relationship that is so exclusive that it is isolating. Also why is his girlfriend the one making these important decisions for him?

But the solution is not for you to make these decisions for him the way your parents did for you. Lay out his options, voice your objections and the possible consequences — and then let him decide.

Raging daughter should prompt avoidance

DEAR AMY: In a four-day visit, our middle-aged daughter (from out of state) flew off the handle over minor matters. This daughter is a control freak who orchestrates the lives of her three young adult daughters and husband. They all operate and apparently thrive on her instant and constant advice.

At our house, she seemed delighted when she was able to humiliate and make cruel and inaccurate statements to us, her elderly parents. It was truly scary to observe her acting calm and loving one minute and then becoming emboldened and excited to tell a humiliating 40-year-old story that criticized her mother. When her fury was over and her mother left weeping, she said, "You know I love you." It's almost as if she enjoys creating conflict. After spending time with her, we're left exhausted and devastated. What should we be doing?

— *Sad Parents*

DEAR SAD: Your daughter might have a rage or personality disorder. Any number of things could be going on. She sounds too volatile to confront, but her problems do not have to become your problem.

When someone is unpredictable, frightening and creates chaos, the most logical thing to do is to avoid being trapped with that person. Limit visits to very short encounters when you have a ready escape hatch; when you've had enough, you can say, "This visit isn't going well, so we're going to call it a day."

Son needs new lesson on what love is

DEAR AMY: My son, who is 19, has been dating a girl for two years. He is very much in love, but this relationship has created problems in our family. Her family is financially fortunate, whereas we struggle just to get by. Recently my husband lost his job, and this has made our lives harder. The girlfriend and her family feel my son isn't good enough for her.

He hasn't the means to buy prom tickets, holiday gifts, etc., but he gives all he has. He has even paid for her dinners and will watch her eat while he eats nothing. It is breaking my heart seeing him feel "less than." We've raised him to believe love is all that matters. Were we wrong?

— *Upset Mother*

DEAR UPSET: If "love is all that matters," then the real lesson is for your son. He needs to learn what love really is.

It is not lovely to eat a meal while your boyfriend has nothing. It is not lovely to expect (or demand) gifts and prom tickets when there are no means to acquire them. It is oh so not lovely to be in a relationship in which you feel "less than."

It is beautiful to be loved just as you are. Your son should be making his way in the world with someone who will cheer him on and inspire him, not deplete and depress him. If this relationship is holding him back, urge him to leave it.

Time to assess why son is friendless

DEAR AMY: My 10-year-old son does well in groups such as Scouts and team sports, but he doesn't have any friends. He's reluctant to invite people over and has started to pull away from the few boys who want to hang out with him.

If this is bothering him, he's not showing it, and he won't discuss it with me. He's a bit of an odd duck, and I'm afraid he'll be picked on in middle school if he doesn't have friends. Is this something to be concerned about?

— *Concerned Mom*

DEAR MOM: This issue is something to be concerned about, but it is not your job to provide friends for your son. Instead, make sure he has the tools necessary to form relationships and make friends.

Some children seem to thrive being part of a group, while others can feel overwhelmed by the challenges and stimulation of maintaining multiple relationships.

Your son may have a quirky and quieter temperament. He may not be adept at reading the sometimes confusing social cues thrown out by pre-adolescent boys, who are experts at creating scenarios of shifting power and alliances.

You shouldn't telegraph your anxiety to your son by querying him about this or pressuring him, but you should speak to his teacher, his Scout leader and his coach. They may report that he does just fine in a more structured peer group overseen by an adult but that he is out of his element on the playground. Or they may suggest he be evaluated for a more serious problem that may be emerging in adolescence.

I admire the work of child psychologist Michael Thompson in describing the inner (and outer) lives of children. I once heard Thompson speak about childhood group dynamics. He said that parents often want their children to have lots of friends, but really, it only takes one friend to make a child feel he belongs. Your son may be a "one friend" kind of kid, and there is nothing wrong with that.

READ Thompson's "Best Friends, Worst Enemies: Understanding the Social Lives of Children" (2002, Ballantine Books).

13-year-old is a model of maturity

DEAR AMY: My 13-year-old daughter is 5 feet 9 inches tall and has had interviews with two well-known modeling agencies, both of which were interested in representing her. Since the interview process, my daughter has gained some weight and is no longer interested in modeling. She said she does not want the stress of always worrying about what she eats.

I respect her for this. She is by no means overweight by normal standards, but she would be for the modeling world. I would never push her to pursue something she is uncomfortable with, but I am afraid that someday she will regret not taking advantage of this unique opportunity.

Should I press the issue in some way or just leave it be?

— *Model Mom*

DEAR MODEL: In my family, we have a little saying when one of our daughters swims against the tide, stands up for herself and makes a brilliant choice: "Give that kid a Buick!"

I intuit that you are the one with second thoughts and regrets about your daughter's decision. Please be careful not to project your own aspirations onto your daughter. She is 13 and has made a good and healthy choice. If a healthy-weight adolescent is too overweight for "the modeling world," then the modeling world is not a world she should live in.

Modeling is not a "unique opportunity." If your daughter chooses this path at some point, she can pursue it. For now, she gets the Buick!

With adult kids, when is job done?

DEAR AMY: I have four adult children, two of whom used to adore each other but now have had a definite parting of the ways.

One of the children has said really hurtful things to other family members, and even after the issue passes there is not one word of apology. Nor have we, as parents, asked for apologies — even when the vitriol is pointed at us.

What are the parents of adult children supposed to do in these circumstances? Stand by and pretend nothing is going on, or try to help work things out? What are our responsibilities, if any, to keep their behavior "between the lines" if they earn their own livings and no longer live in our home?

— *Older But Not Wiser*

DEAR OLDER: When your children become adults, your primary responsibility reverts to checking, monitoring and adjusting your own behavior — not theirs.

Upon reflection, you may see how your behavior has influenced your children. You may see, for instance, how your gargantuan ability to absorb but not react to vitriol condones an abusive dynamic. You may also notice that waiting for "issues to pass" sometimes means that the issue never really passes. It merely lies dormant.

You should not tell these adults how to behave out in the world. You should encourage them to work things out without over-functioning for them.

On your own behalf you say, "I've had it with your behavior toward me. You are my child, and I love you. If you want to talk things out and work things out, I'd really like to do that. But I simply won't put up with being treated badly."

There might be more to this dynamic that you haven't contemplated (or are ignoring). If this adult has emotional wounds left over from childhood, you should welcome these discussions — as long as they remain civil.

Phone bill reveals hidden charges

DEAR AMY: My 24-year-old professional daughter has been living with a man for one year. I pay her cellphone bills. Going through bills, I have discovered that she is talking to and texting another man at all hours of the day.

I don't believe the relationship is platonic because I also discovered (through a package sent to our home instead of to her) that she also spent a weekend with the other man.

I want my daughter to be happy and make the right decisions in life. Should I say anything to her or keep my mouth closed? I have not told my wife or anyone else. It worries me that she will marry the man she is living with but will never be happy. What should I do?

— *Disappointed Dad*

DEAR DAD: This situation calls for a father/daughter conversation. The best setting for this talk would be a diner booth — away from both your homes.

Be honest, be open about your concerns and tell her you cannot live her life for her, but you won't be a party to her dishonesty. Ask, "Do you want to talk about this?" Do not supply answers for her unless she asks for your opinion.

In addition to your compassionate honesty, you can give her a further gift. Tell her you've been paying for her phone long enough. It's time for her to find her own "family plan." I'm not sure why you would keep this from your wife — it's a judgment call, but this seems like a matter she should be aware of.

Grieving parents reach out for help

DEAR AMY: My husband and I have experienced the worst tragedy that a mother and father can experience. We lost our infant son to sudden infant death syndrome. We both fell into a deep, dark depression. Every day continues to be a struggle.

I decided to write to you, to let other parents know that they are not alone in their grief and also to help others provide support to the bereaved parents. A few days after my son's funeral we received numerous cards and flowers, and then everything stopped. We just felt so alone. We still do.

I understand that people do not know what to say. I can tell you that it is better to say something than not to say anything. A simple "I'm sorry" is very meaningful. I hope that you will be able to provide insight on how to approach the parents of a child who has passed away.

— *Mourning*

DEAR MOURNING: My sincere sympathy to your family. Thank you for reaching out to other grieving parents during such a difficult time.

I called Allison Glover, bereavement support specialist for First-Candle.org (800-221-7437). She lost her own child to SIDS 11 years ago and now counsels other grieving parents.

Ms. Glover says she will answer a grieving parent's call any time, day or night (and I can testify that she picked up on the first ring). She wants you to know that this terrible phase will not last forever. "With time you will be able to find comfort and peace. Your lives will come back together.

"There is hope. You should reach out to other grieving families who are a little further along in the journey (you can do this through firstcandle.org or compassionatefriends.org). You may worry that you have outtalked your closest friends and family; keep a journal to express your feelings, fears and dreams."

Most people have unresolved grief, themselves. For your friends and family members: Sometimes words fail, but a mere presence to listen is so helpful. This is especially important after the first six weeks (and certainly during the holiday season).

Glover would like to remind you that even though he is gone, your son will always be a part of your family — and even as you are struggling with your grief, realizing this might help.

'Test tube' baby is all grown up, and in good company

DEAR AMY: I have a son in his mid-30s who was conceived through in vitro fertilization because I was unable to have any more children when his mom and I decided to start a family.

The sperm was provided by an anonymous donor. We chose to keep that secret from my son for obvious reasons. Now, 30 years later, my now ex-wife decided, in a fit of anger against me, to tell him that I wasn't his "real" father (she is jealous of how close he and I are). Someone who witnessed this conversation told me about it. My ex did not elaborate or supply him with any details.

He has yet to confront me. How am I supposed to respond if he asks? Should I bring it up if he acts odd or indifferent toward me? Looking back, were we wrong to keep this information from him?

— *Perplexed*

DEAR PERPLEXED: You should stop acting ashamed of yourself and tell your son the whole truth. Aside from keeping this a secret for so long, you have done nothing wrong. You are his "real" father, no matter what the biological issue. More than 3 million babies have been born through IVF since the 1970s. Your son is in very good company.

Mom constantly hears, 'I love Dad!'

DEAR AMY: I have a 4-year-old son. His mother and I have lived apart for the last 18 months. He spends time equally between the two of us.

For the past few months, he has demonstrated a strong preference for me over his mother. For example, at times when I drop him off at their home, he throws a huge fit, wanting to come home with me. He has also begun saying that he doesn't love his mom — he only loves Dad.

He has even thrown a fit when she picks him up from day care, saying he wants Dad to pick him up or that he wants to go to Daddy's house. I have tried talking to him, but it's not easy to explain that he can love both Mom and Dad when he's so young. I never speak ill of her to him and I even tell him how much Mommy loves him but his response is always, "I love Dad."

I don't think I am doing anything to promote his behavior. Any ideas on what would cause him to act/think this way — or how I can alter it? I know it's upsetting for his mom to hear this, and I hoped maybe it was just a phase, but it seems that it's progressing.

— *Concerned Dad*

DEAR DAD: Let's stipulate that there are no serious issues in the mother's home. If that is true, then I would say that yes, you might be unwittingly promoting this behavior when you respond to a tantrum by talking with him about whom he loves.

It's possible that this is not about his mom. He might be working extra hard to ingratiate himself to you because he's afraid you'll drift away. He needs to know that you are always going to be right where he left you. Reassure him.

The way to help him make transitions is to give him the most stable, predictable and calm environment and to encourage him to try to behave appropriately.

You and his mother should develop a strategy for dealing with this consistently. Make sure there isn't anything going on at her house to make him anxious.

When he freaks out, calmly comfort and reassure him. Say, "Buddy, you're going to be fine. I've got to go but I'll see you tomorrow. Let's go over here and say a nice hello to Mommy and I'll see you later."

Daughter's name belongs to her — to use as she wishes

DEAR AMY: When my daughter was born about 15 years ago, my husband and I decided to give her a lovely ethnic name connected to my husband's heritage. Since then, her original name has morphed into a name that has about 20 different spellings and variations.

I am sorry I saddled my daughter with this problem. No one knows how to spell her name, and even teachers spell it wrong. I always correct the spelling and tell her to correct it, but she feels I am making a big deal out of nothing.

How do I convince her that it is not rude for her to have her name spelled correctly and that she should be proud of its heritage?

— *What's in a Name?*

DEAR WHAT'S: Your daughter may feel that as long as people pronounce her name correctly it doesn't really matter how they spell — or misspell — it. Her reluctance to correct her name's spelling is only really important when it comes to documents such as her passport, driver's license and transcripts.

Because of the unusual spelling, she should be vigilant to correct it on these official documents. Nothing in your letter indicates that your daughter is not proud of her name's heritage, but sometimes teenagers instinctively know what to do battle over and what to leave alone.

You gave your daughter her name, and now it belongs to her. She should be able to choose what to do about it.

Introducing respect to an adult son

DEAR AMY: Our son came back to live in our home three years ago after completing his Ph.D. He has living quarters on the lower level of our home. He is 30 years old, and we feel he should have some privacy so he can come and go as he pleases.

The only thing we have asked of him is that when a friend comes over we would like him to introduce the friend to us out of respect. Are we old-fashioned? He says that when you introduce a woman to the family it is basically saying you are in a serious relationship.

Is this the new rule? What do you think?

— *Curious Parents*

DEAR PARENTS: Your son is referring to a long-established convention: the idea of "bringing someone home to meet the folks."

This implies that a romantic relationship is serious — serious enough, anyway, to travel somewhere for the express purpose of introducing a friend to the 'rents.

However, when you are a 30-year-old living in your parents' basement, bringing someone home to meet the folks doesn't imply anything about your romantic relationship. It simply means that you have wandered into an episode of "Everybody Loves Raymond."

Your son may tell dates that the older couple shouting, "Yoo hoo," from the upper window of his bachelor pad are the caretakers on his modest estate. And you are, in a way. He might be embarrassed to reveal that he is living with Mom and Dad.

I agree that he should show you the respect to introduce visitors to you, but he sounds like someone who has had very little asked of him, and so it is not surprising that he is refusing this small courtesy.

College may be the wrong course

DEAR AMY: I have an 18-year-old daughter. I believe she struggled with learning disabilities (attention-deficit (hyperactivity) disorder, dyslexia and test anxiety) throughout grade school, but these problems went undiagnosed.

During high school, she was tutored three times a week for two hours each time. Despite this help, she got an extremely low score on her ACT test and was unable to get into a college. We tried to get her to retake the test, but she refused.

She went to community college, taking remedial classes for one semester but has now dropped out because "it's a waste of time and money" because she can't transfer the credits to a university. She has finally agreed to retake the ACT, but she refuses to take a refresher class. She needs to raise her score significantly to be accepted by universities. She can't do this on her own. I've seen her take exams, and she absolutely comes unglued.

I have two sons who were easily accepted to their colleges of choice. My daughter has a part-time job, but other than that does nothing from one end of the day to the next. Do you have any suggestions?

— *A Worried Mom*

DEAR MOM: A university education is not for everyone. Your daughter should start thinking seriously about a profession. One of the advantages of community college — aside from the cost and convenience — is the access to practical professional training. You should stop pressuring your daughter with intensive tutoring and college-entrance testing and pursue an accurate evaluation and assessment.

This will be helpful, but she still will have to take responsibility for her own life, including coping with her challenges. If she balks at community college right now or can't commit to any particular path, she'll have to increase her work hours. Working hard and making money will help her to feel (and actually be) successful.

Unacknowledged gifts reveal painful family secret

DEAR AMY: When I was 17, I had a baby. My parents adopted my child, "Barry," and I moved on and married when he was 2. Now my parents are deceased. Barry knows the truth. He has two children and considers me to be their grandmother.

I send cards with money on minor holidays, and I send more gifts and money on birthdays and Christmas. None of these gifts is acknowledged. Before Christmas I took three large garbage bags filled with gifts for his kids, along with money for him and his girlfriend. I never even got a call from them on Christmas.

Should I scale it back? They never call unless he needs money. My husband says to cut it back and just send a few things on Christmas and birthdays. Barry does not have much money, and we are fixed pretty well, but we have three kids and three other grandkids.

I love Barry and his family, but should I say something to him about the lack of acknowledgment? My brother says guilt is driving me to do all of this gift-giving, but I feel I have to. Amy, what do you think?

— *Unsure*

DEAR UNSURE: I agree with your brother. You cannot purchase a healthy relationship; you need to scale this back dramatically. You should let "Barry" know that you have started a college fund for his children; beyond that you should give the kids one gift each on their birthdays and Christmas and all of the love, affection and attention that you can spare.

For couple, last names come first

DEAR AMY: I have a very slight problem. My wife and I have been married for seven years. When we got married, I didn't care whether she took my name, and she didn't ask me to take hers. (I wouldn't have.)

We have blissfully retained our individual identities for our entire married life, and it doesn't bother anyone in the slightest. My wife and I have a child, with another on the way. While she was gestating our first, we discussed last names and quickly realized that neither of us was going to be happy with his or her last name relegated to the exile of being a middle name or any other decision that favored one last name over another.

The result is that we hyphenated the last name. Our daughter now has a first and middle name to go with a hyphenated last name that's of considerable length. This seems grossly unfair to me. We have saddled our children with the consequences of our inability to compromise.

As they grow, our children will undoubtedly lament the length of their last name. I can't even begin to contemplate the possibilities for when they get married. At one point we discussed a hybridization of our last names, but the most natural way to accomplish this includes my complete name and only a part of hers, which seems unfair as well.

Any advice would be appreciated. Also, any anecdotes from readers about the ups and downs of having long and/or hyphenated last names would be great.

— *Conflicted Father*

DEAR CONFLICTED: This problem is only slight if you think names aren't important, but obviously you (and your wife) believe that names are the only window onto one's identity. So you need to answer this question: Who can claim primacy to your child's identity — you or your wife?

OK. That was a trick question. Your child's primary identity belongs to the child. So far, your child, whom I will call "Brittany Clovis Stevenson-Glockenspiel" is mainly the symptom carrier for her mommy and daddy's unwillingness to identify as anything other than their individual selves.

One way out lies in the symmetry of your growing family. You could give one child your surname and the other your wife's. This keeps everything fair, with each of you clinging to your separateness.

Or you could read this letter back to yourself and notice (as I did), that you are a very smart person locked in a sad and silly conflict. I also take issue with your characterization of a middle name as being some sort of identity exile. Maybe because I love my own.

Because you wrote to me, I vote for your name to go in the middle.

Questions of death bring on child's sadness

DEAR AMY: I have a granddaughter who is 5, and one day while we were on vacation, she and I were sitting together, and she started to ask me if I am going to get old.

I told her that we all get old, and that is why we have birthdays. She broke down crying, saying that she didn't want me to die and that I had to promise her that I would not have any more birthdays.

It took us more than an hour to get her calmed down. She is dead-set against anyone having any more birthdays. She also said she didn't want to have any more birthdays after she turns 6. Because of this I did not let them write "Happy Birthday" on the cake when my birthday rolled around.

Is there some other approach we can take so she doesn't get upset?
— *Ontario, Canada*

DEAR ONTARIO: Death is a profound issue and definitely something to get upset about, especially when you're 5. You cannot and should not avoid this. You should have reassured your granddaughter calmly without resorting to a promise that you won't celebrate your own birthday, for goodness' sake.

This merely reinforces her fears that birthdays are somehow dangerous and to be avoided. If this comes up again, assume the role of the wise granny. Hold the girl close and say, "There, there — everything is fine. I'm not going anywhere any time soon."

Dad questions at-home nudity

DEAR AMY: I am the father of two boys and a 3-year-old girl. My wife is concerned about my daughter seeing me naked when I change clothes or shower.

Growing up, it was never an issue to see my two brothers, mom or dad nude. My wife has a sister and never remembers seeing her dad naked when she was growing up. My wife has a very bad and negative body image, and I don't want my daughter to be that way.

What age is recommended for a daughter to stop seeing her father naked and vise versa? I want her to grow up healthy mentally.
— *Not Bashful Dad*

DEAR DAD: Every family is different, as your story illustrates. And while body shame is not a good thing, body privacy is.

There is a real difference. Shame is when you hide your body because you are afraid of or ashamed of it. Privacy is when you keep your body private because it belongs to you and you might not want to share it by having other people look at it.

Generally, 3-year-olds are starting to become aware of their own bodies and their body parts. Your daughter should be taught the correct names for her body parts and for yours, her mom's and her brothers'.

At around her age, she should also start to learn that her body is her own and that she has a right to keep it private (this is what her mother chooses to do) if she wants to. Privacy doesn't translate into a bad body image unless your daughter is taught that her body is something to be ashamed of.

Although I think it's perfectly OK for your daughter to see her dad and brothers nude, as she grows older you should be aware of and responsive to her own sensitivities. If your nudity embarrasses her — even if it doesn't embarrass you — then it's time to wear a towel.

Parental queries bring on stepmother's pain

DEAR AMY: I am a stepmother of two beautiful, amazing children, ages 9 and 7. I have been a part of their lives for many years and I count myself as one of their four parents (my husband and me; their mother and her husband). The problem is the rest of society.

Since my husband and I married several years ago, the question from his family, my family, friends, co-workers, etc. is when we are going to have our own children. We always say that we already have two children and every time, the other person always says, "Yeah, but it's different with your own."

To any stepparent who is loving and involved, this is incredibly hurtful and ignorant. This sort of statement would not be made toward an adoptive or foster parent — so why should a stepparent count as anything less?

— A (Step)mom

DEAR (STEP)MOM: I understand your frustration and appreciate your advocacy for stepparents. I have one quibble, however. You say that people would never question that adoptive or foster children are "real" children — but people do question this, all the time.

Stepparents are "real" parents; adopted children are "real" family members, and other than for points of clarity, I don't see any reason to distinguish between people in families related by DNA or by choice.

A 'Grammie' by any other name would be just fine

DEAR AMY: My son is 31 years old and has had only two serious relationships. He has been seeing a co-worker for several months and she has moved into his home along with her two children (they are ages 3 and 16 months).

I am very happy my son has found someone who makes him happy. My question concerns what these children should call me? They call my son by his first name. I am not comfortable having them call me grandmother or any other form thereof, or any cute made-up name. I would rather they call me by my first name, but my son and the children's mother prefer they call me some reference to grandma. What do you think?

— *Jane*

DEAR JANE: While this issue sometimes seems trivial on the surface, it is important because it has to do with identity.

It would be one thing if you were insisting on being addressed as "Grandma." You are not. You are asking that you be called by your name. Why is this unacceptable?

The inconsistency is confusing. It is OK for the kids to address your son by his first name, but you have to be "Grammie"?

This domestic situation seems to have progressed quite rapidly, hence the confusion. Marriage might clarify matters for everyone. This is relevant because if they had taken more time, everyone (including the kids and you) would have had plenty of time to figure out how to be addressed.

I agree that the children should call you by your first name.

Siblings

. . . .

They Know You Like Nobody Else,
and That's the Problem

Pushover tests limits of sisterhood

DEAR AMY: I have a sister I love dearly except for one thing: She is a total pushover when it comes to her kids. Her oldest son is 38 years old, lives at home, has no job, runs all night and sleeps all day.

He has three children by two women that he is not supporting in any way. Lately, he has brought a new girlfriend into the mix, her new baby (by another man) and her dog that pees all over the house. My sister has a daughter (32 years old) who also lives there with her daughter and her dog as well. And my sister has a dog.

None of these ingrates contributes to the household expenses. We have the same conversation over and over again, and I just can't do it anymore. She refuses to throw anybody out, especially now with the weather getting cold.

I say make them responsible for themselves. I have tried all the avenues I can think of to help. I just hate how they take advantage of her, but I hate even more how she lets them. Any advice?

— *Disappointed Sister*

DEAR DISAPPOINTED: Your sister has it within her power to live her life completely differently, but she is making choices every single day that put her at the center of this dysfunctional, chaotic household. You need to assume that despite what she may say to you, her family system is cranking along pretty much the way she has designed it to, and that this pattern goes way back to her kids' childhoods.

You don't actually say if your sister is unhappy with this state of affairs or if you are mainly unhappy for her. The only thing you need to do differently is to stop having the same conversation over and over. I give you permission to stop offering solutions that she has no intention of enacting.

You can be her concerned and loving sibling simply by responding: "I'm so sorry you're unhappy and frustrated. This sounds really tough." Do not offer one more suggestion until she says these words: "I can't do this. I want my life to be different. Please help?!" Then you can pull out all the sisterly stops to advise and assist.

Close sister makes girlfriend jealous

DEAR AMY: I am jealous of my boyfriend's sister, and it causes me such anguish. I don't like feeling this way.

We have a long-distance relationship and see each other every four or five weeks. We talk every day on the phone and email, etc., but I get jealous when he spends time with her. She lives nearby, and they are very close. They spend a lot of time together, especially when she is between boyfriends. To make things more complicated, he is separated and lives next door to his wife.

I realized today that I am jealous because he gets to have emotional support, whereas I am alone and do not pursue close relationships with other men. My siblings do not live near me, and I'm not close to them, anyway.

I have tried to tell myself not to care. It's not that I fear it is a romantic situation, but when he was really sick recently, she took care of him. They spend weekends together. Once I went to visit him, and he invited her to join us on an outing! Please help me put this into a healthy perspective.

— *Grappling Girlfriend*

DEAR GIRLFRIEND: First of all, your guy isn't quite divorced. If he were divorced, it might remove the doubt and insecurity that's settling round you like a fog.

It seems that you are jealous not only of the specific person he has a relationship with, but of the relationship itself. So the answer here is for you to do the hard work required to develop close and supportive friendships of your own. The more secure you feel, the less pressure you'll place on this man to fulfill all of your emotional needs. Given the distance between you, he simply can't provide everything you want.

A word to the wise: Your guy's sister is not going away. You should get to know her on your own — through Facebook, email, etc. If you have a friendship with her (independent of your mutual connection), your jealousy will dissipate and the fog will start to lift.

Teen ponders reporting friend's brother

DEAR AMY: I am a teenager. I have a friend, "Hattie," who is going through a rough time at home. Her brother has dropped out of college, and he is back at home, dealing drugs instead of getting a job. Hattie told me, but she is in denial.

Should I report him to the police? I am afraid that he will harm her. A few days ago he had a terrible argument with his mom, and it got violent. Hattie isn't a weakling, but she is physically smaller and mentally insecure. But if I do rat him out, will my friendship with Hattie be over? Will I later regret it?

— Good Friend

DEAR FRIEND: What you can offer your friend is perspective — and a very supportive friendship. I agree with you that this situation sounds volatile and frightening. You should talk with your parents or another trusted adult about the best course of action, including perhaps inviting her to stay with you. Police will not always leap into a situation based on what a third party reports, but you could also try to get advice from them about what Hattie should do.

In this family, enabling runs amok

DEAR AMY: My sister's husband is an alcoholic. He makes half-hearted attempts to get treatment, and then goes on another binge. When he's drinking and gets verbally abusive, my sister shows up at my place to crash for a few days until he's sober again.

This has been going on for years. I love my sister, and I will always be there for her, but I am getting fed up. Whenever she shows up at my door, she says she will leave him. Then she goes back and tells me he has apologized, he's getting treatment — and then the whole cycle replays itself again and again.

I know she is "enabling" him by not giving him an ultimatum and not moving out (her finances are tight, but since she is paying their rent now, I know she could afford a place of her own). Am I enabling her by letting her crash on my couch time after time? Do any of your readers who have been through this have any advice?

— Fed Up

DEAR FED UP: You are "enabling" your sister. Your availability as a crash pad provides an escape hatch, not only from her domestic emergencies but also from her anxiety. It also helps her delay making a tougher decision. You, basically, are part of this marriage's system.

If you want out, tell her so. Ask her, "What would you do if I wasn't here? What would you do if you didn't have any other place to go until your husband sobered up?"

Tell her you don't want to be involved in her marriage any more and that it's time for her to find another place to live so she can move out for good. Take her apartment hunting. I don't think you should turn her away, but you should make it more uncomfortable for her to fall onto your couch.

I'm sure readers will share their ideas.

Dog has automatic anxiety detector

DEAR AMY: Whenever I go to my sister's house, her dog jumps on me and scratches my legs. My sister insists I'm to blame for the dog's behavior because the dog somehow senses I'm nervous in its presence.

She says that if I'd just relax, the dog would leave me alone. I disagree, as I feel it's the owner's responsibility to train a dog not to behave in this manner. Who is right?

— Scared Sister

DEAR SCARED: You and your sister are both right. Dogs have an amazing ability to detect human anxiety, and they react by being agitated or by trying to charm the person into submission. However, no responsible pet owner would allow her dog to assault a visitor.

If her dog jumps on you, your sister should protect you and discipline the dog. She sounds unwilling to do either. You might broker a peaceful solution by asking her to show you what you should do when this happens. Many dogs respond to a code word or command ("Down, Muffin!"), which achieves results.

Sibling closeness leads to shared invitations

DEAR AMY: My brother and I have many mutual friends, share several interests and enjoy one another's company. We are both in our 20s and, because of the economy, we both live at home with our parents.

I am single, and he is in a long-distance relationship. I understand it when strangers jump to the conclusion that my brother must be my boyfriend.

What bothers me is that some of our mutual friends treat my brother and me as though we are interchangeable — as if a message to one of us will reach the other one by default. We have received Christmas cards and party invitations addressed to both of us.

I never answer for him or do anything else to encourage this, and my brother and I have always given separate gifts and sent separate cards. What else can I do to make it clear that I want to be treated as a distinct individual?

— *Not My Brother's Keeper*

DEAR NOT: You could try to announce an official separation, but the fact is that until you two move out of your family's home and on your own, you will be lumped together as family members.

I don't think there is anything wrong with you two sharing a party invitation or Christmas card if you share a home address and friends.

You will simply have to continue to emphatically correct friends when they assume that you speak for your brother, saying, "Let me give you his number. You should give him a call."

Sisters differ in response to grief

DEAR AMY: My sister and I have been relatively close throughout our lives. She is 63 and I am 58. Both of us lost our spouses in the past year.

She continues to grieve and I have moved on (with therapeutic help). She calls me at least two times a week. We are both retired. She was left well off and I am struggling but I make it. She has few hobbies, interests or friends and starts her day reading the obituaries. She is bitter and wallows in her grief.

Now she wants me to move in with her. I don't want to but don't know how to tell her without creating a lasting rift. I love her but I don't like her very much. Can you help me to find the words?

— Sister

DEAR SISTER: No two people grieve the same way. You cannot assume your sister will recover from her loss the way you have, but you could help her by reflecting her actions back toward her and offering to be helpful and emotionally supportive, without becoming a crutch.

Speak your own truth, with respect and compassion.

You say, "I know you are going through a very rough patch and I'm so sorry. I think there are things you could try which might help you to feel better. Would you be open to some suggestions?"

Your sister might be afraid to change — or she might simply be unable to pull out of her sadness and grief. I hope you can offer her a positive example, including suggesting therapy. You can respond to the idea of living together by saying, "I don't want to move in together but we'll always be close." You don't need to explain why. You need only say, "I have to do what I think will be best for me."

Sister issues demand for elaborate baby shower

DEAR AMY: My sister has a son who will be 3 in June. She is due to have a second child in April.

She wants to have a baby shower but wants my mother and me to put it on for her. It may be acceptable in some places, but I have never known anyone to have a second shower, and I feel people would think it is not appropriate.

My sister and I are not speaking because of this. I had even suggested having a couples shower or diaper party, but that wasn't good enough for her. She wants a full-fledged shower. I feel like it is ridiculous for her to almost demand this, but now I don't know what to do.

— Frustrated Sister

DEAR SISTER: Your sister might see this shower as your family's obligation to treat her second child with the same elaborate welcome with which you welcomed the first.

Many women are enjoying/demanding second showers, but these events are usually less elaborate than the party for the first child. You should assure your sister that you will love and indulge her second child as much as you do the first, but if she doesn't wish to participate in the event you're willing to host, perhaps she has a friend who will do as she demands.

Declawing kitties inhumane

DEAR AMY: My brother's long-term, live-in girlfriend and I care about each other very much, but we are both hot-headed and stubborn. I recently agreed to foster a mother cat and her kittens. I have grown very attached to them. I also am anti-declawing. My brother and his significant other have decided to adopt one of the kittens; they are excellent caretakers.

She wants to have the kitten declawed. I am 100 percent against this, believing it to be both unnecessary and cruel. She doesn't want the cat to "wreck the furniture, scratch her children or destroy their expensive speaker system."

I pointed out that the adoption contract (which has not yet been signed) does not allow declawing and states that a declawed cat will be defaulted into the shelter's ownership. She said she was going to have the cat declawed anyway.

I have agreed to take back the kitten any time if her claws become an issue. How can I prevent the declawing of this cat without causing a rift? We are all attached to each other and to this kitten.

— *Foster Mom*

DEAR FOSTER: Declawing cats is inhumane; there are many ways to mitigate scratching without declawing an animal. If you release this kitten into the care of someone you know will have its claws yanked out, you are in breach of your agreement with the shelter. I can't imagine the shelter would use you to foster cats in the future. If you can't effectively persuade your brother and his girlfriend not to do this, blame the shelter's policy. If they want house pets with no claws, they should get an ant farm.

Daughter gone for days at a time

DEAR AMY: Six years ago, my parents adopted two children from Russia, a girl and a boy. The girl is now 18 years old. She is a junior in high school.

For the last few months, she has been treating my parents' house as if it were a hotel. She will leave for school in the morning and then not come home for days at a time. My parents do not know of her whereabouts during these times.

After however many days (the longest was a week) she will show up back home, promise to do better, and the very next day she takes off again. My mother is at a loss as to what to do, and my father just throws up his hands. They no longer suspend privileges as they did before she turned 18, and they won't punish her either.

The sixth time she left, they dismantled her bedroom and she now sleeps on a mattress in the basement, when she chooses to show up at night. I realize that she is an adult and is legally able to make her own choices, but I feel that she is using my parents because she knows they won't make her sleep on the streets. My mom has told her she will always have a bed at their house.

It is very frustrating to see this. I think they should make her shape up or ship out. Your thoughts?

— *Frustrated*

DEAR FRUSTRATED: Your parents cannot make your sister shape up. They can make her ship out, of course, but they have already announced that they will not bar the basement door.

Rather than throw up their hands, your parents should do everything possible to get help for your sister. She was 12 years old when she was brought to this country; she could be struggling with mental illness, drug use, an attachment disorder or emotional crisis brought on by or exacerbated by trauma in her early life.

Older adopted children face many challenges — and some families adopting from Russia have dealt with cases of hidden physical, emotional and mental illness in the children they have adopted. Urge your parents to research the possible causes of your sister's distress.

She should be checked thoroughly by a physician who knows her adoption history. Your folks also should reach out to other parents of adopted children for support and resources. An organization called Families for Russian and Ukrainian Adoption might be a good first step: frua.org.

Your parents must try to help your sister while protecting the rest of the household from the chaos she brings into it. To ignore her problems now represents a second abandonment.

Sister's out-of-control drinking causes family crisis

DEAR AMY: My sister lives in another state with her husband and three children. When my sister drinks, she drinks until she is blind drunk. She is a good mother as far as keeping up a nice home and helping the kids with homework, etc.

Her husband is an enormous help with the children. He has a lucrative income and provides a beautiful home and whatever the family needs. He has begged her to get help, and he said he would stand by her forever, but she is in total denial and has become indifferent to him.

Her husband seems tolerant of her abuse and puts up with it because he fears for the children. He has had to call the police twice. He is afraid that some day she may drive with the children in the car while under the influence. Her family is in denial and will not confront her. What can anyone do?

— *A Troubled Sister*

DEAR SISTER: If your brother-in-law feels trapped in the home because he fears for the children, this is a sure sign that he should act in their best interest, put their safety and well-being first, and consider separating.

Generally, that moment when you find yourself calling the police on your spouse is a sign that your "beautiful" home life is out of control.

You can't make him act, and you can't make your sister stop drinking. What you can do is express your concern about behavior you personally witness (i.e., "Sis, I am very worried about your drinking. Over the holidays you became quite belligerent. Your drinking is out of control, and you need to get help to stop."

You can offer support to your brother-in-law and the children. At the very least, he should look into attending Al-Anon meetings (al-anon.alateen.org).

Dating

· ·

It's Not for the Faint of Heart

Disinterest isn't always game-playing

DEAR AMY: I have been seeing a guy I went to high school with. Lately we've been hanging out. We seem to have some common ground. We talked about what we were looking for, and I said that I wanted a relationship. At first, he said he did not want a serious relationship, but then he said he wanted to take things slowly and see where things went.

He told me he was not the type to play games. Since then he has not texted me or called at all. If we do communicate, it is because I text him. I do understand he is busy (going to school and working), but I just don't know what to make of all this. He is a great guy, I really like him and we have a lot in common. I just don't want to waste my time. What do you think?

— *Confused in College*

DEAR CONFUSED: This guy told you he doesn't play games — and he isn't playing games. He simply is not interested in having a romantic relationship with you. If he were interested, he would initiate contact. You've been honest and straightforward. Good for you. Now you should move on to develop a relationship with someone who is interested in having one with you.

Lucky woman is double-dating

DEAR AMY: A week and a half ago, I went on a first date with a great guy. We spent a long lunch getting to know each other — the date lasted five hours! We've seen each other a few more times since, and I really like him. Not five days later, a friend of a friend asked me on a date, and we also had a great time. Now I have two awesome men in my life, both with their own unique qualities, but I'm feeling guilty for dating two people at the same time!

What should I do? I really don't know either of them well enough yet to decide whom I like better or whom I would be a better woman/girlfriend/wife for. I've expressed to them that I'd like to take my time getting to know them, but I'm getting messages from them both daily. I don't want either to feel rejected, and I don't want to be callous with their feelings.

How long can I keep this up? How do I decide?

— Divided on Dating

DEAR DIVIDED: It's called "dating" for a reason — you are getting to know people. You can tamp down your guilt by being honest with both men, even though at this early stage it's really not their business whom you are seeing (they may also be seeing other people). Nor at this stage should you worry too much about what they want in a woman/girlfriend/wife. Your job is to focus on what you want.

Girlfriend took a walk on the wild side

DEAR AMY: I have been dating "Connie" for six months. She is by far the best girlfriend I have ever had. She is comfortable in her own skin and accepts me as I am. She is very kind and understanding, unpretentious and a lot of fun to be with.

This week we discussed living together. For the first time, we discussed our sexual histories. She told me that for almost two years she experimented with many sexual situations — some of them quite wild and extreme, certainly in my mind. Connie didn't excuse her behavior. She said that she did what she did because she wanted to, and that this is in her past and she will not engage in those practices again.

I am confused by her previous behavior and more confused by my own feelings. I really love her, but this revelation bothers me. I told her that. She said that who she is now is based on her life experiences, and that she can't undo the past. She said she wants a monogamous relationship with me.

Amy, I am sure you have more experience than I do in this area. Are there any clues for sorting out my feelings?

— Anxious Guy

DEAR ANXIOUS: Thank you for assuming I have experience walking on the wild side. (At my age, fantasizing about things that didn't actually happen is about the most fun I get to have.)

I do know about feelings, however. Feelings get sorted out, one painful moment at a time. Your girlfriend is right about many things — including that the entirety of her experiences makes her who she is. She sounds authentic, likable and honest.

I suggest that you two sit down and discuss every aspect of her sexual past that you are curious about, and that you try not to blame her for behavior she doesn't regret. Of course, you should both also be tested for STDs.

Monogamy is a choice your girlfriend sounds eager to make. Trust is a choice too.

When exes email, should she reply?

DEAR AMY: During my time in high school and college, I had some tumultuous relationships with men. Most cheated, were verbally abusive or were emotionally absent. I loved one of them in particular, but the rest were mere infatuations. These relationships left me heartbroken, and it took several years to heal from the damage that had been done.

I have not maintained any contact with any of these people, however, all of them have sent me messages through social networking sites within the past one or two years expressing regret and guilt over their treatment of me. A few even wanted to know how I was doing and hoped to have a friendship. I declined to respond.

I have no desire to give any of these exes the time of day, not to mention a reply that signifies forgiveness and/or friendship. I have been in a healthy and loving relationship for the past four years, one that is on its way to a marriage, and I do not want to threaten it in any way.

However, I feel that I am holding back on granting possible closure for these men, who may have grown up in the past six or seven years and want to right the wrongs from the past. I fear that contacting them would open up several wounds that took very long to heal. What do you think I should do?

— *Hesitant*

DEAR HESITANT: You say you don't want to forgive these men, and, given your attitude about forgiveness, why should you care about their getting some kind of "closure?"

You should imagine that the mere act of reaching out and making whatever conciliatory statements they are making might be closure enough for your exes. You could easily reply to these messages with an innocuous statement like, "Thank you for getting in touch. I'm doing very well and wish you all the best."

Otherwise, if you feel that replying at all would place you or your relationship at risk, then by all means leave it alone and move on.

Chaotic home life a problem for kids

DEAR AMY: Six months ago, I got drunk and woke up in bed with another man. My fiancé was yelling at him. It has been hard, but I quit drinking, got counseling and made it my purpose in life to be a better mother and partner. I'd been unhappy for years because my fiancé never goes anywhere with me. If we go out, we go separately because we don't like to hire baby sitters for our two kids.

Now, my fiancé has come back from a work trip where he had a weeklong affair. All the evidence was on display to find, but when I confronted him, he said it was a mistake, not an affair. I asked him to leave, but he refused. The police have said he doesn't have to if he doesn't hit me.

His mistress has told me he is only staying with me for another couple of weeks. She says that he is crazy about her. My fiancé and I fear commitment and divorce. We sit in limbo, afraid to get married or separate. Last time we talked about it, he said he does want to get married. I don't know what to do.

— *Sober but Confused*

DEAR SOBER: Do you really think this mess boils down to your refusal to leave your children with a baby sitter? The way you portray the atmosphere in your home, the kids might be better off with a sitter.

Now that you are sober, you should focus your energy on staying sober. Ask your counselor to help you explore your choices and their consequences, and ask your fiancé to come into therapy with you. Your primary commitment should be your children. You could repair your relationship, but until you do, a peaceful separation may be best for the kids.

Solo vacationer may return home to empty apartment

DEAR AMY: My live-in boyfriend and I have been in a relationship for 2½ years. We just took a vacation together. A week after we came back, he informed me that he was taking another week's vacation in one month to the Dominican Republic. And he said he is going alone.

I am hurt that he made this decision without taking my feelings into consideration. He says he hates the cold weather, has the money and time, and is going regardless of what I say or how I feel. I am jealous of the time he will be spending talking and hanging out with other women while he is there. I feel that this is not a good thing for a person in a committed relationship to be doing.

Sometimes I don't think I can take this hurt and don't know if this is going to destroy our relationship. What do you think about this?

— *No Tan Lines*

DEAR NO: It doesn't bode well when people in committed relationships make singular pronouncements without discussing their ideas or plans ahead of time.

There is nothing wrong with partners vacationing separately, but this should be a mutual decision. Your guy is going, so let him go. You don't have to act happy about it, but don't be a basket case, even if you feel like one.

While he is gone, make some decisions about your relationship. He decided he was going on vacation alone, and you may decide to go it alone after that.

Loving couple want wall between them

DEAR AMY: My boyfriend and I have been dating for almost five years. We are middle-age, well-educated and financially secure. We are deeply in love and completely committed to each other.

Between us, we have four children from previous marriages. His two are out of the house, and my two are teenagers. He rents an apartment, and I own my own condo. We would like to get married but have put off getting engaged because we are both fiercely independent. We enjoy spending time with each other, but each of us has lived on his/her own for several years now, and the thought of trying to mesh our daily routines is hard to swallow.

As fate would have it, another condo has become available for purchase next door to mine. If he bought it, we could get married and then be free to spend as much time together as we see fit. My boyfriend and I love this idea! Those closest to us think this is a great idea for us, but there has also been some skepticism to this rather "modern marriage." I would be interested in your thoughts, as well as those of your readers.

— *Ms. Independent*

DEAR INDEPENDENT: For those of us who have occasionally fantasized about moving into the garden shed, if you two went ahead with this living arrangement, you'd be living the dream.

I know two married couples who have lived in neighboring apartments for at least a portion of their marriage, and both said they loved it. You should talk about the living space and domestic activities and duties you will share. Because of your adjoining lives, you should meet with a financial counselor before marriage to discuss how joined your finances would be.

I'd love to hear from readers with unusual marital habitation arrangements.

Love bites in mysterious ways

DEAR AMY: I was in a relationship with "Steve" for about a year. Then one day, while we were still together he showed up at work with another woman. They both had hickeys on their necks, and they were holding hands. One of my friends/co-workers confronted them, asking if they were dating, and the woman said, "Of course!" I was devastated.

Several months passed, and then I finally got the courage to talk to him about it. He told me he was stupid to do it, that he had messed up badly, and that he would like another chance. I gave him that chance, and a couple of months later, his ex-girlfriend got out of jail. He broke up with me again — this time for her.

She has a bad reputation for messing with people, so I told him, "If she breaks up with you again, don't bother coming back." Now he's acting really sweet and saying that I'm the only girl on his mind and that he wants the two of us to work things out. He says he has messed up but he wants to change.

Amy, my feelings for him burn like the heat of one thousand suns. I feel as if I'm completely lost in a forest of love. I want him back, but I don't want to be hurt again by the man I love. What should I do?

— *Lost in the Forest*

DEAR LOST: "Steve" certainly has brought out the poet in you. And because you can't see the love forest through the trees, I will supply the next act of your romance for you.

You will take him back. After a honeymoon period ranging between a couple of hours and a couple of weeks, Steve will walk into a bar sporting matching hickeys and holding hands with another woman — or some version of this. You will be devastated, and the next time he is between girlfriends he'll beg your forgiveness.

You will cycle through this relationship with him until you wise up. You could save yourself the inevitable devastation if you would imagine this scenario, walk through it in your mind, and decide to skip it altogether.

Secret rekindling casts doubt on relationship health

DEAR AMY: About six months ago I left an abusive husband. We have one child together. I have one from a previous relationship and he has two from a previous relationship. I have my children with me.

I have been seeing and talking to my ex for a couple of months and he seems to be changing. He wants me to go to counseling with him and he wants me back. My parents and friends do not know I have been seeing him.

Most of the time he is a great person to me and other times he is very mean verbally. Is the fact that he wants me back a sign that he wants to control me? Or is it really love between us? Is he really trying to change? Does he really want to be together?

— *Confused and Nervous*

DEAR CONFUSED: I left my relationship "Magic 8" ball at home today, so I don't know whether your husband really loves you and is ready and able to change. However, my own guess is "Outlook not so good."

The key here is the fact that you are keeping this renewed relationship a secret from friends and family. You are keeping it a secret because you know they will be upset and concerned. I suggest you discuss this with the people who know you best and let them guide and counsel you.

Do not commit to anything and do not get too involved until your ex proves — over a long period of time — that he has changed. You could start by seeing a counselor with him but you should be extremely circumspect.

To wait or not — that is the question

DEAR AMY: My first real relationship was when I was 18. The relationship got serious quickly, but I still made him wait several months before sleeping with him.

Now I'm 22 and on the brink of a new relationship. I'm wondering, is it a sign of immaturity if I make a guy wait a longer time than the couple of dates they're used to waiting now? I know it's all about "when I feel ready," but do men find it respectable when a girl makes them wait, or does it seem as if she's taking a relationship too seriously and therefore acting immature about it?

— *Confused*

DEAR CONFUSED: According to you, it could be a sign of maturity if you have sex with a guy after two dates and a sign of immaturity if you wait to have sex. I understand that you think guys want girls to be casual about sex. But just as you have an idea of what you want your sexual and emotional life to be like, many guys do too.

Sex is not a game, and "making people wait" is not necessarily a gauge of maturity. If mature people don't want to have sex, they choose not to have sex. A couple in a serious relationship will discuss this — frequently. Sex means different things to different people, and men and women often interpret and react to sex (and the idea of sex) differently.

In my experience, people often regret having sex. They seldom regret waiting to have sex. Your only job is to always act according to your own values.

Man ponders place in adulterous affair

DEAR AMY: I have been having a same-sex affair with a married man who has two children. Now he says the affair is over. He says he is staying in his unhappy marriage because of the luxurious life he has. His in-laws are socially well-connected.

He told me that he told his wife before they got married that he had been with men, and yet they still got married. He told me he has cheated with other men, especially during the time when his wife was pregnant.

He asked me to have unprotected sex with him at his home. I did not do this, but I worry about his wife and her health — and her sexual health. He at some point will give her an STD or worse — infect her with HIV.

What should I do? I feel she needs to know what her husband is up to, but I worry. Is it my place to say something?

— *Worried*

DEAR WORRIED: You didn't wonder about whether it was "your place" to have an affair with a man you knew was married, but now you're worried about what your place is? Now that you've violated the very basic standard that says it's wrong to have an adulterous affair, you should tell this wife what you know about her husband.

If she knows her husband has relationships on the down low, then your notification might not have much impact. If she doesn't know, then she should be told so she can decide what to do concerning her marriage, her family and her sexual health.

Social anxiety makes partying hard

DEAR AMY: My partner and I have been living together for four years. We have a good relationship. We rarely fight or argue, and are basically compatible and for the most part happy. The one area that is a problem for us is in the social arena.

My partner has social anxiety. When we attend parties or other social events together, he is extremely anxious, shy and awkward. It is painful for me to know how uncomfortable he is at these events. Consequently, I cannot relax and have a good time, either.

I now turn down invitations because these events are so distressing for him. We have discussed anti-anxiety medication, but he is opposed to it because of the sexual side effects. I can't say that I blame him. I am not a social butterfly, but I do like to go to a party once in a while.

I am wondering if it is OK for couples to socialize separately. If so, how would I tell the host that only I will be attending and how would I answer the inevitable queries from others at the event concerning the whereabouts of my partner?

— *Feeling Left Out*

DEAR LEFT OUT: You don't mention that either of you is a physician. While it is responsible for you to consider all of the options, dismissing a possible treatment because of possible side effects is putting the first course before the appetizer.

Your partner should start by seeing a physician and also a therapist, who could assess him, recommend medical and nonmedical strategies for dealing with his anxieties, and chart his progress. Practicing in smaller groups could help him build on modest successes. He could keep a diary to note how he feels in specific settings, then look for patterns.

There is nothing wrong with socializing alone. You could tell the host that your partner sometimes feels uncomfortable in groups. If you want to fudge, say he has other plans and sends his regrets, but emphasize that you look forward to the event.

Wait for the seasons to change before talking marriage

DEAR AMY: My boyfriend and I have been together for about a month or so. He has two kids, and I have a child as well. We've known each other for more than three years; there has always been a spark between us, and now that we're together I'm so happy. I can see myself marrying him, and he has the same feelings about me. My question is, is it bad that we have all these plans after a month of dating? I love him so much, and he loves me too.

I'm just not sure how my family would feel about our plans after being together for such a short time. And if they oppose our marriage, how can I explain it to them to help them realize our views on this?

— *Love Struck*

DEAR LOVE: You two are happily in love. Good for you! Enjoy this. Revel in it. But don't discuss any marriage plans with your family until you have been together long enough to see at least one season change.

You don't say what your mutual romantic histories are — or how old your children are — but this is an opportunity for both of you to do things right with the goal of getting things right. Doing things right means being respectful, careful, judicious, kind and caring. It means talking, talking, talking about your values and demonstrating positive values to all of your children.

If your children and extended families see you making such an effort, they should be delighted to learn that you two want to marry. In fact, they may suggest it.

Boyfriend scarce after the 'L' word

DEAR AMY: I'm a 25-year-old woman. My boyfriend of six months is 28. This past weekend we went on a short trip together. Something happened that I cannot seem to get out of my head.

We had a few drinks and he proceeded to tell me that he loves me (we have said the "L" word before); he also said that he would marry me in a week and that he wants me to have his baby. I just sort of laughed this off but decided to ask him what he remembered the next day.

Amy, he didn't remember any of it and now he's avoiding me! I love this man and I'm not sure what to do.

— *Upset*

DEAR UPSET: Either your boyfriend is a blackout drunk, or he's embarrassed by his admission and avoiding you rather than discuss it. Either scenario doesn't bode well for your future as a couple.

You have attempted to face this thing head-on by trying to talk about it, and he is responding by running for cover. And so you have to ask yourself: Is this what you want in a partner? Back off and see what he chooses to do and then you can be the one to decide whether to run toward or away from this relationship.

Boyfriend chooses to cohabit with nudes

DEAR AMY: I'm a 25-year-old woman and am in a great long-term relationship with a very nice 27-year-old guy. Everything about him is great. About a month ago he moved into a loft apartment with two other guys about his age, who have been living there for a few years. The setup is very nice: It's in a great location and very reasonable. His roommates are generally very gracious and creative young men.

The problem is the decoration in the loft. It's full of images of naked or almost naked women. Some are fine art prints, but others are just raunchy pornography. Some are centerfolds; another is a headless female mannequin wearing nothing but lingerie.

I don't feel comfortable visiting or hanging out there with so many women being displayed like that. I asked the girlfriend of one of the roommates what she thought of the mannequin, and she said it was funny.

My boyfriend has told me he does not want to upset the new apple cart by moving in and demanding that they change the apartment around. I don't want to come off as a demanding prude by saying they should redecorate their place, so what should I do?

— *Grossed out Girlfriend*

DEAR GIRLFRIEND: Like you, I wouldn't want to hang out in a porn palace, but presumably this stuff was on the walls when your boyfriend chose to live there. He isn't willing to represent your point of view to his roommates. Your only other option is to react to this decor yourself.

These men hung this imagery on their common walls for a reason. You can assume they enjoy it enough to explain it to someone who is willing to challenge their choices. When and if you get to know them better, you can say, "OK. I'm dying to know. What's with all the nudes?"

If they say they "love the human form," you can tell them you've got a vintage Playgirl centerfold of Burt Reynolds you'd be happy to present to them. Otherwise, if you can't adjust to this I suggest you steer clear.

Emotional extortion harms this loving couple

DEAR AMY: I have a heart-wrenching decision to make about giving the love of my life a second chance. He will not be honest with his two children about our relationship. His 16-year-old daughter and son (age 20) have told him that if he marries me, they will cut him out of their lives and never speak to him again. His ex-wife is fueling this and has so far been successful in making his children think they have the right to make this ultimatum.

This is emotional extortion. He is currently serving in Iraq. He and I have been living together stateside. His children and his ex-wife find this unacceptable. During a visit home recently he asked his son to help him move some personal belongings out of our apartment to put them in storage. This was a sham gesture to make the son think we are not together.

I was so upset I ended the relationship. I am humiliated and devastated. I think he is spineless. By phone today he said, "I will be honest with my children about us," but I've heard this for more than two years. Should I give him a second chance?

— Devastated

DEAR DEVASTATED: The important people in your guy's life are pressuring him, and he is reacting by scurrying for cover. Because he has essentially moved out of your home, your "second chance" could be to dial back your relationship and calmly continue to assert your choice to live authentically.

A good parent models appropriate and mature behavior. Allowing his kids to jerk him around isn't good for him — but it is really not good for the kids. His ex is training them in the art of emotional extortion, and he is permitting it.

When he comes home, if you two want to be together permanently, you can decide to get married (living together without marriage creates doubt about your relationship). If he is honest, patient, happy and in charge of his own life, his kids should come around.

Long-distance relationship is not progressing

DEAR AMY: My boyfriend and I have been in a long-distance relationship for nearly two years. He used to be very loving and affectionate. Now, his sweetness and affection have waned significantly (though he still wants to have sex).

I've brought this up and tried to revive some affection on my own, but without any luck. He says that things change over time. He says I have changed, becoming too clingy and trying too hard! He still says he loves me and sometimes talks about our future (other times he says he feels pressured). I'm getting mixed signals. I love him dearly, but I don't feel the love in return. It's become a huge point of contention. I see glimmers of hope in some words and actions and then he shuts down.

I can be somewhat over-emotional, especially when stressed, but he used to be much more caring, compassionate and understanding — helping me work through these things. Now it only frustrates him. Part of me wants to wait it out to see if it's just a rut. Another part of me wants to cut ties now and try to retain a civil relationship (since we share many mutual friends). I'm 23, he's 28, and we only see each other on the weekends. What do you think I should do?

— Love-Stuck

DEAR STUCK: Your boyfriend is correct when he points out that "things change over time." Things do change — and when a committed couple love each other, things often change for the better.

You should make any decisions about your own future based on the idea that your boyfriend will remain remotely affectionate and slippery when it comes to commitment. The only thing you can do is also the best thing to do, which is to work on your own behavior. You sound eager to push this relationship into permanency, and your boyfriend's actions indicate that he is just as eager to avoid it.

Stop pushing, and he might stop pulling away. I realize that asking you to stop being needy, anxious and over-emotional is a tall order, but if you can marshal your own strengths and confidence, you'll receive more from the people who love you — and you'll stop settling for less.

Insane attraction part of toxic cycle

DEAR AMY: I fell into my first complicated relationship. The story is typical: We dated, broke up, got back together, broke up again, and now we are starting to "talk" — again. This has been over a period of one year.

The reasons we have broken up in the past are many and varied. He was the one to initiate the breakup both times. He has also initiated getting back together, both times. We have not slept with anyone else in between our breakups, and despite the reasons we broke up, we have common interests, have fun together, are comfortable and could talk for hours. We also have insane physical attraction.

Although I don't wish to get back together with him (at least right now), both he and I don't want the "cut and dry" separation we need in order to move on. I am emotionally tired from the pain and his constant change of mind and heart, but with each push and pull, the insecurity of parting gets to us.

Our relationship was never out of control or abusive when we were together, and I am his first serious girlfriend. He has let me down on events that were important to me. But then he becomes sweeter and more understanding. We are like each other's drugs. Should I maintain the romantic relationship that we have and enjoy the moments, or break it off for good?

— Jaded

DEAR JADED: You say your relationship has never been out of control or abusive, and yet your description of this relationship, which may at times seem exciting, makes me anxious to the point of giving me hives. I think it's giving you hives too.

This is not healthy. You are not enjoying it. You two may have insane physical attraction, but with you the emphasis is on the "insane." Your boyfriend exhibits some characteristics of an abuser. Letting you down, breaking up and then charming you back into the relationship establishes an unhealthy cycle. Even if this isn't abusive in the strictest sense of the word, it is definitely an emotionally unhealthy roller coaster for both of you.

I think you need to break it off. For good.

Apologize and your relationship may be rewarded

DEAR AMY: Over a year ago, I broke up with my boyfriend. We had been together for 18 months. We started dating after I graduated from college. I was overwhelmed by entering the workforce, shocked by the transition away from friends, and living in my parents' basement.

He was finishing his senior year in college more than 200 miles away. We were each other's first long-term relationship, and in many ways we were a great couple.

We tried to make things work, but the distance between us, insecurity, jealousy and eventually deceit came between us. After our breakup, things turned ugly and painful. He was hurt by my words and actions. He decided to take a job overseas on a two-year contract, and he has been away for almost a year.

I had a somewhat wild streak. I dated many people and threw caution to the wind. Now I am in a more stable situation. My feelings toward him continue to grow stronger, and my intentions are more genuine. I'd like to reach out and contact him (via email is the only way), but I am unsure of how to even start the conversation. I'd like to mend this relationship. Is this even possible — or worth it?

— Unsure

DEAR UNSURE: Any relationship is worth mending. You should contact your ex to apologize for your actions and ask him for his forgiveness.

Don't swing for the fences. Tell him you've grown up a lot and that you have many regrets for how things ended between you. Tell him what you're doing and how you're doing, and ask him a couple of questions, which you can hope he will answer by clicking "reply."

'Friends with benefits' yields neither

DEAR AMY: I have been dating a man for three years whom I met through an online dating service. I am 65 years old and a widow. He is 68 and divorced. He has told me that marriage is not his goal but that he would marry if the person were the "right one." We dated for a year but then my job forced me to relocate 90 miles away.

He did not like this but decided to try this long-distance relationship. We have had a lot of ups and downs and distressing situations. We see each other every weekend, alternating driving to each other's location. This works fine for me, but he doesn't like it. Last year I found out that he was back on the dating service network. I felt betrayed. I told him the relationship was over.

He begged forgiveness and wanted to try again with the thought that maybe I would relocate to his area. I accepted this plan with some skepticism. Now we are in a relationship that he classifies as "friends with benefits."

A few months ago he told me that he intended to go back to an online dating service to find the relationship that he had wanted all his life.

Without announcing it to him, I then enrolled in a dating service and guess who they matched me with? Him! Now he is angry and says I deceived him. I feel like a jerk. He said, "I know you care about me, but not enough. Why don't you ask Amy's opinion? She will tell you that you don't understand relationships and have not been honest with me."

So now I feel terrible and my self-esteem is shot. What do you think?

— *Sad*

DEAR SAD: The term "friends with benefits" implies that you two have a friendship and a sexual relationship unfettered by exclusivity. This doesn't seem to be working. Evidently you do not offer him the "relationship he has wanted all his life." He has every right to look for this relationship.

When he joined a dating site without telling you, you felt betrayed. You then did the same thing — and he feels betrayed. Goose? Meet gander.

If you were joining this dating site to retaliate, that is silly gamesmanship. However, if you were joining the site to find the relationship you have wanted all your life, then godspeed. Next time, choose a different database.

Woman uses an idiot to get over a jerk

DEAR AMY: I seem to have found myself wanting my horrid ex-boyfriend back. I thought I loved him, but in reality I was just obsessed with him. There was no "me" time. It was as if I didn't even exist. I don't know why or how it happened, except it was my first sexual relationship.

Now I am dating a great guy; he's kind of an idiot but great, nonetheless. I don't think I love him, and I don't think we have a future.

My ex is a complete jerk. Unfortunately, I still want to be with him. I know we're not good for each other, but I also know that my current boyfriend and I aren't any better. I know I'm just using him to stop loving my first love, but it's not working.

What do I do?

— Help

DEAR HELP: Has it occurred to you to be alone for a while?

Think about it: no Jerk No. 1 or Idiot No. 2 — just you and your couch and the Lifetime channel. (Not that you should take your relationship cues from the Lifetime channel, mind you.)

You cannot use one person to get over another person. As much as I wish it weren't so, idiots and jerks do not cancel each other out. Idiots and jerks accumulate. What you need to change is not only the company you keep, but your ability to keep your own company. Be alone. Figure out what you need to do differently. And then do differently.

Before sex, have a heart-to-heart

DEAR AMY: I am 80 years old. I have a male friend who is also 80, and we have been enjoying each other's company for more than a year. A while ago, he told me he has had another friend for a long time and he was having trouble giving her up. Meanwhile, our relationship has progressed.

I think they see each other from time to time for several days at a time. I am not sure what type of relationship they have, whether they are just friends or bed partners. I would like to know where that relationship stands as compared with the one he and I have. Our relationship has progressed to a point that I am very uncomfortable sleeping with him if he is sleeping with another woman.

I have another male friend who would like to have a sexual relationship with me, but I just don't feel right about it. I don't know how to deal with this situation. What do you suggest?

— Confused

DEAR CONFUSED: There is an alarming and growing incidence of sexually transmitted disease among older people. According to statistics compiled by the Centers for Disease Control and Prevention, almost a quarter of all Americans with HIV/AIDS are older than 50.

This reality should help you achieve some clarity about a situation that carries emotional and physical risks for you — and this man's other partner — as well as any other partners you might have. You two must have a frank and careful discussion about this.

If you do not want to be in a relationship with him while he is seeing someone else, and if he won't alter his behavior or use a condom, then you should make the difficult choice to — at the very least — cease your sexual relationship with him.

Never been kissed? Get out and flirt

DEAR AMY: I am a 21-year-old woman who has never been asked out, gone to a dance, been kissed or flirted with a guy in my entire life. I grew up in small towns and never had any lack of friends — but they were all girls.

I was involved in a lot of activities, and I was perfectly happy without a significant other. I wasn't interested in any of the boys I went to high school with. I was sure I would find a nice guy when I went to college. I didn't.

After college I moved to a big city, and I still haven't met anyone or been asked out. I'm wondering what is wrong with me. I know of a lot of girls who are about as attractive as I am who have been in several relationships.

I'm tall (5 feet 10 inches tall), so that may scare some guys away. I wear makeup and exercise regularly. My hair is usually neat and I wear clothes that fit and are attractive.

What is wrong with me? Why don't any guys like me?

— *Never Been Kissed at 21*

DEAR NBK: If you believed what you saw in the popular media, you'd think that the world is populated by bodacious Kardashians and their boy toys. Not so much.

I think your situation is more common than you know. You do not need to remake yourself into something you're not, but if you want to attract a guy you should put yourself out there in a way you haven't been.

Men and women are very similar in that both sexes respond well to "flirting." People are attractive to others when they are open, confident and friendly.

Ask your women friends to give you feedback about how you look and behave when you are around guys. Are you outgoing and receptive? Do you maximize your best assets? Ask for help and learn to flirt — even a little. Engage in coed activities you enjoy. Practice as you go.

Rules on dating with an age gap

DEAR AMY: I am an almost 30-year-old man, and I recently resigned from my job. On my last day at work, an 18-year-old co-worker cornered me and kissed me. She told me that she is very attracted to me and said if I wanted her, she'd be mine.

We worked very closely together for the past four months and had gotten quite close as friends. The attraction is mutual. I find her to be a charming and beautiful girl. My concern is the age difference. I worry about how people will respond if we enter a relationship.

My friends are divided — some say that I need to follow my heart, and others say that I shouldn't even be thinking about dating an 18-year-old. Am I wrong for thinking about entering into a relationship with this girl?

— Uncertain Suitor

DEAR UNCERTAIN: The red flags I see flying over this scenario are not only about the age difference between you two — but about her behavior.

If the genders were reversed in this situation, and it was an 18-year-old man who "cornered and kissed" a 30-year-old woman, I'd suggest that somebody might want to get the police involved.

Her behavior is so aggressive that you only need to imagine what she might do if you dated and then dropped her. (Picture her perched in a tree and yelling into a megaphone outside your apartment.) Take all of this into consideration, and if you still want to dip your toe into this pool of crazy, I say you two are (presumably) adults.

Ask to see her driver's license to verify her birth date, check the laws of consent in your state, make sure her father's not the angry type, shake the bushes for high school football player boyfriends, be prepared to have at least one conversation about Miley Cyrus, and go for it.

Reader asks if people can change

DEAR AMY: I recently left a two-year relationship with a man who has anger issues as well as family issues from the past that he never properly dealt with. We fought for months before I finally ended it.

I left him because our fights started escalating to the point that he would grab or shove me to try to get his point across; alcohol was involved every time this happened. I realized that this was wrong and that I was unhappy, and my friends have commended me for leaving him.

He has since gone to see a counselor to deal with his issues, including his drinking. I have not spoken to him since I ended the relationship. He has written me several letters telling me his counselor has helped him do some soul-searching. He says he knows that the way he was reacting to me was completely wrong, he has gotten his drinking under control, and he wants another chance to show me that things can be better.

I do love this man. Everything else about the relationship and his personality were a perfect match, but I am afraid that if I give him a chance we will fall back into the bad pattern we had before. He is a smart person with a great job. I encouraged him to talk to someone to deal with his personal issues so we could have a healthy relationship that could possibly lead to marriage. He has finally done so, and that gives me hope.

Even so, I find myself wondering if people ever really change. Do they? Should I give this person one more chance, or should I move on?

— *On the Fence*

DEAR ON: If I didn't believe in change, I'd give up on my diet and continuous spiritual quest, retire this column and finally sleep in.

The most prudent way to gauge someone else's change is to trust, but verify. I don't think it is enough for this man to get his drinking under control — he should stop drinking. It will take more than some soul-searching sessions with a counselor to effect permanent change.

At the very least, you can acknowledge his efforts. If you want to renew a relationship with him, be prepared for resistance from friends and family — they will worry about you. If you do this, reviewing your troubling relationship history with him and his counselor would be wise.

Let him go before 'expiration date'

DEAR AMY: I have been dating a great guy for a year and a half, but he recently decided to pursue his dream of moving 1,000 miles away to attend graduate school. He is leaving in three months, and we do not plan to continue with a long-distance relationship after he is gone.

A month ago, I met someone new. Under normal circumstances, I would never consider breaking off my current relationship or dating someone behind my partner's back. However, my current relationship has a definite expiration date on the horizon. Am I wasting my time by waiting around for my relationship to run its course? Or would it be selfish to end things now? I care very much about my partner and would hate to hurt him, but is it time for me to move forward?

— *Torn*

DEAR TORN: I don't know if it is time for you to move forward. You obviously want to, but you seem to want assurance that this will be easy, prudent and low-drama. Breakups don't generally work this way, even when there is an "expiration date."

Breaking up now would only be seen as "selfish" if you truly believed that the prospect of your boyfriend spending another three months with you (while you watch the clock waiting for the relationship to end) would be a lifetime gift to him. Your partner is acting in his self-interest to leave town, and you can act in your self-interest by supporting his choice and letting him go — just a little sooner than later. Just don't be sneaky about it.

Relationship lapses feed depression

DEAR AMY: I've been in a purely sexual relationship for a couple of months. I suffer from anxiety and depression. A few times in the past months we've stopped talking to each other. During those times, I have severe depressive episodes.

She makes me happy, and I've been told I make her happy. My friends tell me that I shouldn't continue this way, but I'm happy. I'm conflicted on what to do.

— *Conflicted*

DEAR CONFLICTED: Being in a sexual relationship releases endorphins — this is part of the "chemistry" that people often feel when they connect with each other. This chemistry masks your depression and anxiety, but it doesn't treat or cure it.

The roller coaster of attention and distance you describe in this relationship isn't good for you because you don't have the resilience to tolerate it. In fact, it could amplify your anxiety and depression and make your symptoms worse. Stability is what you need, and this relationship (at least the way you describe it) doesn't offer it. I agree with your friends that this isn't good for you.

You should concentrate on developing the tools to cope with your personal challenges; this is tough because working to tackle your own issues means committing to a long and sometimes lonely path. But once you are stable and content in your own life, you will attract people and relationships that nurture you — rather than offering temporary patches.

Love affair brings on tough choice

DEAR AMY: I think I found "the one." He's funny, ambitious and we communicate seamlessly. Unfortunately, he lives half a continent away (we met while traveling through South America). We talk every day, and we've managed to meet up once a month for the last eight months. Every visit has been perfect.

I graduate from college this spring, and he's asked me to move to be with him while he finishes medical school, but I'm not sure! I'm worried that I could find a better job somewhere else. I would hate myself for moving if we broke up in a month, and it was all for nothing.

It feels like I could never love anyone else this way, but I'm only 22, and we've never really been together while not traveling. Should I follow him, or am I living in a fantasy? Should anyone my age follow a boyfriend? If I followed him, could I respect myself as a modern career-oriented woman?

— *Kate*

DEAR KATE: No experience in life is "all for nothing." The period immediately after college is a rare time of life when you can make a relatively low-stakes choice to live wherever you want to live, and then move if you want to.

You may have misread the modern feminist concept, which is not to negate your personal life in favor of a career, but for you to be your own person. You should do what you want to do.

Can you find a job in your field in your friend's town? If so, go for it. My only caution would be for you not to live with him. Modern relationships demand intentional behavior, and for you to truly be your own person, you should be self-supporting, independent and able to build a life outside of your romance.

Type A girlfriend in love with goals

DEAR AMY: I am a 21-year-old female, and I've been dating my 25-year-old boyfriend for more than a year. It's a very healthy relationship. We get along very well. We haven't discussed marriage or children because we both feel we're too young.

My parents raised me to be an extremely hard worker. They taught me to set goals and to achieve them. My parents taught me that I could do anything I wanted to, as long as I worked hard enough. With that mindset, I'm extremely successful. My parents are proud of me, my boyfriend is proud of me, and I am proud of me.

My boyfriend is not as goal-oriented as I am. He does not care to work hard to achieve his goals. In fact, he no longer sets goals. I've tried to talk to him about setting goals and achieving them, but he seems to think that his goals will not be met, and so he doesn't set them.

I truly love him. However, his lack of drive is something that will be an issue if we decide to stay together. I can't change my views on working hard because it is extremely important to me. Can this issue be mended?

— *Worried*

DEAR WORRIED: This can be mended, but only if you change. There is nothing "wrong" with operating as your boyfriend does. Not everyone is driven, a goal setter and achievement-oriented.

You and your guy have different temperaments. You two might be perfect complements to each other just as you are, except that you don't want him to be the way he is. You want him to be the way you (and your parents) are.

The way to mend this would be for you to respect your differences. Even though ultimately this might be very good for you as a person, you declare that you can't do this (nor do you want to), and so for long-term success you'll probably have to find someone else who is more like you.

Amy's rules for getting over an ex

DEAR AMY: I've read your column for years, and now I want your advice. I am a freshman in college, and a couple of months ago I was dumped by my first boyfriend. We weren't together very long, but I am still hung up over him. Winter break has ended, and I'll have to see him; I don't know how I am supposed to feel. How do I get over him?

— *Breakup Hang-Up*

DEAR HANG-UP: It occurs to me that I have been writing this column for more than half of your life. And I've lived the whole "how to get over him" question for far longer. How are you supposed to feel? Exactly the way you do feel. However, how you act can have an impact on how you feel, and to some extent, you can consciously "act" your way out of this.

When I was your age and going through this, I was so freaked out, I fell over from nerves in front of a former object of my affection. Please — do not do this. But forgive yourself if you do.

Model your behavior on the coolest person you can think of. Avoid your ex, but prepare yourself for those times when you'll run into him. Do not fall over. Stand tall. Act cool. Stuff down the drama, and act neutral. Self-medicate only with the warmth of your friendships and Nora Ephron movies. Plunge into your schoolwork and extracurriculars. Do not drink. Erase his number from your phone.

Spring will come, and by the time the lilacs are in bloom, you will feel better.

Suspicious boyfriend should choose to trust

DEAR AMY: I have been in a serious relationship with my girlfriend for over a year now. Our relationship has been strong because we seem so good for each other.

My girlfriend revealed that several months ago, she had a conversation with an ex. It was not sexual, but he was a big part of her life for a long time, and she felt the need to have a conversation with him regarding her feelings. I don't like that she waited several months to reveal this. I had made it clear that I wish to know about any dealings with him, and she lied to me for months through omission.

Since the time she came clean, I have lost some trust. I looked through her phone several times to see if they have been continuing their conversations. She occasionally looks through my phone too, and I don't have a problem with that because I have nothing to hide.

I saw there was a text conversation between them recently. It was platonic, but she hadn't mentioned it to me. I now realize she feels my looking through her phone is a violation of privacy (even though she looks at mine). I respect this and won't do it again.

There is now an underlying resentment on both sides. I would hate to see what is an otherwise wonderful relationship be ruined because of this. How can I help resolve this in a healthy way?

— *Insecure*

DEAR INSECURE: Honesty, disclosure and transparency are important, but you need to decide: Is any contact with this ex a deal breaker, even if you know your girlfriend is not reviving a relationship with him? If so, you better make it crystal clear to her. And if the relationship is over, then how many conversations must they have before they run out of things to say to each other? She needs to disclose her intentions.

You must then do a very challenging thing: Choose to trust. Tell your girlfriend, "It's obvious that your contact with him hurts me. I'd like you to keep that in mind." After that, stay out of each other's phones. With no evidence of cheating, this surveillance seems more like a trigger than a cure.

Daughter must choose between her family and forbidden love

DEAR AMY: I am a 19-year-old college student. I date on rare occasions. My father has raised me to be open-minded and to look for a guy who makes me feel amazing, unless he's African-American (I'm white). My father is racist and has said to my face that he will disown me if I become committed to a man of that race.

The older I become, the more I am attracted to black men. I want to respect my father and live up to his expectations (and that of my extended family, who share his ideology). But is it right to follow my heart and date whomever I choose?

—*Unsure in South Carolina*

DEAR UNSURE: I think of your attraction as an understandable, inevitable reaction to the deficit of reason, logic and old-fashioned family values in your household. Denying your right to date whomever you want to date forces you and your family into an ancient dance of forbidden love (for cultural references, read about Tristan and Isolde, Romeo and Juliet, Miss Piggy and ... everyone).

If you choose to date a man whose skin tone is too dark for your family, you must understand that this is high-stakes behavior on your part. Though some families are transformed by being forced to face these issues, you should assume that your family is actually capable of following through on their threat to cut you off completely. Follow your heart, but prepare yourself.

Divorce

· ·

Ex Marks the Spot

Ex-husband exhausted by ex's drama

DEAR AMY: I had my last drink one year ago. Since then, my life has been transformed. In the process, I have been divorced, met a beautiful woman and got engaged. Now we are expecting a blessing in the form of a baby!

My ex-wife has not fared so well. Her drinking has spiraled out of control. She has been arrested for domestic violence. After getting arrested, she called me to bail her out because she was "too embarrassed" to call her father. The next day, she drank heavily and called saying that she was going to commit suicide. I jumped to the rescue on my white stallion, calling friends that were near her so that she would not have a chance to succeed. She was placed in the psych ward of the hospital. Her dad took her out before any therapy could start. She said she was unwilling to be "stuck in the nut hut" because there is nothing wrong with her.

The drama has increased lately. She still controls parts of my life through emotional blackmail and guilt. I was not the best husband, but how much do I have to do to make amends for that? I can't seem to get away from the tornado that is my ex-wife. How do I tell her that I want nothing more to do with her?

— *Stuck in Her Wake*

DEAR STUCK: You are not helping your ex-wife by rescuing her into the control of family members who enable her to keep drinking. You help her the most by offering to support her only in sobriety.

The next time she calls you from jail, you should leave her there rather than release her to immediately resume her drinking. She desperately needs rehab, and she might receive it only if forced by the court. Her life is on a dangerous downward spiral. The message you should send to her is, "I care about you. I'm terrified for you. But I will only support your efforts to get clean. When you are ready to get sober, I'll take your call." This is the toughest part of tough love.

Married couples often travel in pairs

DEAR AMY: I have two sets of married friends whom I've been close to for more than 20 years. We all live in the same neighborhood and are all friends, traveling together and spending vacations together, etc. I got divorced five years ago and am now single. These two couples do a lot of things together without me, which is fine.

However, lately it seems that I get left out of celebrations when I used to be included. Recently, the four of them went with another couple to the mountains to celebrate one of their birthdays. I was not invited. And then, for someone else's birthday, they all had dinner together. I was not invited.

I try to be open to us all socializing as we please, and I tell myself that we all don't have to be together all the time, but I can't help but be hurt when I get left out. Am I being overly sensitive?

— *Left Out Friend*

DEAR LEFT OUT: Married couples are like loons — they seem most comfortable with members of their own species.

However, you should examine your own behavior. Do you host events, invite your friends to your home and remember their special occasions? This exclusion could be a sign that you need to take more initiative.

This situation has put you in the uncomfortable position of revealing your own vulnerabilities to try to affect a renewal of your friendship. So tell them, "I know we don't have to be joined at the hip for every occasion, but I miss being with you and want to make sure you're not excluding me because of anything I've done."

Divorced student hides early marriage

DEAR AMY: I got married when I was 18 to the man I had been with since age 15. Our marriage lasted for a year and a half, and we ended up separating. Our divorce was finalized last year.

Now I am 22. I'm in college, making new friends and having a great time. I have a boyfriend. I'm in love with him, and we live together. I feel I can't tell anyone about my past. I'm worried that people will look at me differently. I feel embarrassed that I already have a failed marriage in my past.

I have no regrets, really, but I just hate being 22 and divorced; it's like I failed — and in the worst way. My boyfriend knows about it and says it's not a big deal. I haven't told my closest friends because I'm afraid it will change the way they look at me. I just want to know how I can get over this and not let my past get in the way of my present and future.

— *Regretful*

DEAR REGRETFUL: If you have no regrets, then why all the secrecy about the reality of your life? It's OK to have regrets. Most people's lives are punctuated by at least a few.

The idea is to make sure you own your regrets, admit your mistakes, learn from your experiences and live an authentic life. Your life does not have to be perfect. You shouldn't have to harbor a secret from people who know and like you. If your marriage was a mistake, then say so. Who knows, someone else might learn from your experience.

You don't have to make a big announcement about your past. Let this come out naturally. Be honest. Friends tend to share stories about previous relationships. You should share yours.

Significant other becomes insignificant

DEAR AMY: I have lived with my significant other, "Martin," for 16 years. We own a house together. The past few years, I have tried to tell him we were growing apart, but he never believed we were.

Recently, a woman he dated 30 years ago e-mailed him. They began an online and phone relationship. While he and I were visiting my family, he said he was visiting cousins in another city when he was actually meeting her at a motel. Within a month, they decided they were going to dump their partners.

He finally told me about her and even proposed having her come to the house to identify what items she would like to have that we jointly own.

Amy, he does not believe he did anything shameful. He justifies all his actions by saying they are in love. He has yet to apologize for his conduct or admit that any of it was dishonest or dishonorable, and now he says that since I said we were growing apart it made him vulnerable to her overtures.

What do you think of his conduct?

— *Disgusted*

DEAR DISGUSTED: "Martin" will not admit to any wrongdoing and will not apologize. I agree that his behavior is reprehensible. Rather than try to force him to make statements he will never make, you should contact a lawyer and begin the process of separating your property. Let your lawyer do the talking about how to dissolve your common-law marriage (if this status is recognized in your state), and do your best to move on.

Stop saving your wife and start saving your life

DEAR AMY: I need advice concerning my breakup with my wife of 30 years. My wife has a very serious drinking problem. She has been on diet pills for more than 25 years and also abuses prescription pain pills. I have tried numerous times over the years to get her the help she needs, but she refuses. Our family doctor has also tried to get her to recognize her problems, but to no avail.

My wife recently had me removed from our house; she went to court and lied about me, saying I had threatened her. I know it's the alcohol, and I've attended Al-Anon meetings to try to understand the issues. If she doesn't want to help herself, what am I to do?

— *Devastated Husband*

DEAR HUSBAND: You seem frantic to help your wife but, according to you, you have tried absolutely everything and nothing has worked. You should consider your wife's alcoholism a tragic, progressive and (in her case) possibly terminal disease. Then you should accept your own inability to treat or cure it.

You have been forced out of your home. It is time for you to concentrate not on saving your wife but on saving your life and rebuilding what's left of it. Al-Anon will help. You also need legal counsel as well as emotional support.

Husband was seeing men on the side

DEAR AMY: After 20 years of marriage and three children, it turns out that my alcoholic husband is gay. He has been with literally dozens of men over the course of two decades. In the meantime, I have been a dutiful wife and good mother who never saw it coming. I have divorced this man, and I am picking up the pieces of my shattered life. My oldest child (18) knows the truth; the two younger ones, ages 9 and 12, do not.

Currently my "ex" is sleeping with a married man who also has children. The wife of the man he is involved with is a close friend of mine. Should I tell her? Also, when, if ever, should I tell my younger kids the truth about their dad? He will not tell them, and so I have to decide what to do.

— *Distressed*

DEAR DISTRESSED: You should tell your friend what is going on, and you and she should be tested for STDs.

You should also tell all of your children a version of the truth now and leave the door open for further talks. The fact is that if their dad is involved with someone your family knows well, there is every possibility the truth (or a rumored version of it) will circulate in your community and possibly their school.

You should disclose their father's alcoholism. His drinking is not an excuse for his actions, but might explain some of his behavior. Tell your kids you are worried about their dad and that you hope he will get some help. Say he has a lot to work out. You can say, "He decided he wanted to be with other people instead of just me and that's why we're getting a divorce."

You should disclose their dad's sexuality when you think they're old enough to understand it. They may hear about this and figure it out, so it's best if you truthfully answer all of their questions and then do your best to be honest, calm and reasonable when you are with them. This is a tall order when you are hurt and betrayed.

Your entire family would benefit from talking with a counselor, together and separately — because each of you will respond differently to this challenge.

Nude ex-wife still hanging around, sorta

DEAR AMY: My husband of five years has a painting of his ex-wife (who is posing partially nude) that he displays in our home. He says that it is just art and that he paid a lot of money for it. Am I wrong to feel disrespected and to want the painting to go away?

— *Not an Art Lover*

DEAR NOT: In my book, unless it is the Renaissance and you are a member of the House of Medici, all family portraits hanging in the home should be A: of actual family members, and B: fully clothed.

You describe your residence as "our home." If this is in fact your home, then you should have veto power over what is displayed within it. Because your husband is an art lover, I suggest you find a local art student who would be able to give you a low-cost "family portrait" of your own.

I won't suggest the obvious — that you supplant the portrait with one of yourself. Instead, supply the artist with a photograph of your ex (I assume you have one). Depict him with long, flowing hair astride a horse with his shirt ripped open the way you see on the cover of romance novels.

This painting should be the same dimensions as the one of the ex-wife. Hang them side by side. This will backfire if your husband loves your ex art as much as he does his ex art.

Wife wants husband's ex to back off

DEAR AMY: My husband's ex-wife continues to telephone, text and e-mail him, even after he has asked her many times not to.

She walked out on the family 10 years ago, and until I came into the family, she had his ear on "kid problems." Those kids are now grown, married and have children of their own. He doesn't feel the need to discuss anything with her, yet she continues to pester him!

We've been married for a year and a half. I sense the "I don't want him, but I don't want anyone else to have him either" thing going on. The children deal with her on their own terms. I think she has told them that I won't let him communicate with her and that I am the reason he "can't be civil" to her. Should I speak to her myself? What more can my husband do? He has made it clear he wants nothing to do with her!

— *Help!*

DEAR HELP!: I suggest that you are, in fact, the reason your husband "can't be civil" to his ex. Your husband isn't a child. Surely he knows that he can "pester-proof" his life by not responding to his ex. But please remember that civility (at a polite distance) should be the goal between ex-spouses. You could mitigate some of your jealousy and also keep an eye on things by also being civil to your husband's ex.

Divorcee's family should be more sensitive to her

DEAR AMY: I was divorced a year ago after 19 years of marriage. It is still difficult for many reasons. Even though I am having a hard time, my family has insisted on continuing a close relationship with him. In fact, my sister and her family are taking a trip with my former husband, his girlfriend and our daughter. I feel it is far too soon to be taking my daughter on a trip with his new girlfriend.

My family knows my feelings and knows this is extremely hurtful to me but they see nothing wrong with it. My mother actually said to me, "I don't see the problem — you're divorced." What am I missing here?

— *Sad*

DEAR SAD: What you are missing is a family that is willing to step across the divorce divide and be on your side. One of the unfortunate aspects of divorce is how it affects all family relationships. Family members sometimes have to establish and maintain some emotional and actual distance from people they are otherwise very fond of.

The way you portray your family, they are announcing that they are unwilling to make these changes or even acknowledge that this is difficult for you. They want their friendship with your ex to continue unfettered and unchanged.

Your ex-husband is also unwilling to establish boundaries with your family members for your comfort. To include your ex-husband on family vacations while they are excluding you is disloyal to you. I assume there are other factors at play, but I agree with you that this is inappropriate, mainly because it makes you very unhappy.

Wife's affair brings on trust issues

DEAR AMY: My ex-wife and I split about a year ago because she had an affair, and now I have deep trust issues. My fear of being hurt again and the lack of trust has caused me to push my girlfriend away multiple times. I want to be a better person, the person I used to be, but every time I have a chance to prove it I squander the moment.

I'm afraid that it may be too late, but I want this relationship to work. What can I do to change my behavior and prove myself to her?
— *Sad and Stuck*

DEAR STUCK: The solution for you lies partly in making conscious and rational choices not to make your girlfriend pay for someone else's behavior.

You say you want to prove yourself to your girlfriend, but the person who really needs proof that you are worthy of lasting love is you. You can "behave" your path out of this by moving slowly and having successful experiences with your girlfriend that you both feel good about.

You've been out of your tough marriage for only one year. Tell your girlfriend that you want your relationship with her to work out. Ask for her patience as you learn how to make the choice to trust again. Trust is the greatest gift, but first you'll have to really believe that you are worthy of this treasure. And then you'll give it to yourself.

The trouble with 'no-fault' divorce

DEAR AMY: I have been putting off a divorce for far too long for various reasons. I have been married for 25 years. My wife had an affair early in our marriage, and we worked things out with counseling. Two years ago I caught her having another affair, but for family and health reasons I did not divorce her at that time.

We put on an act for others, including our two children, so no one knows how bad our marriage is. Now my kids are in college and I want a divorce. My kids love their mother dearly, and she is a good mother.

Even though I am seething with anger under the surface, I do not want to do anything to hurt my children but I also do not like lying. I also don't want them to somehow blame me for the divorce if I don't tell them the real reason. We have a lot of family in town that we see often.

My question is, What do I tell family, co-workers and, most important, my children about why we are divorcing? My wife certainly does not want to tell anyone that she is an adulterer, but that is not my concern.

— *Soon to Be Ex*

DEAR EX: In the old days, the injured party could legally charge a cheating spouse with adultery. The concept of "no-fault" divorce obscures the fact that frequently there is fault.

Given the absence of charging your wife or forcing her to wear the letter "A" in the town square, the only question you need to ask yourself — and answer honestly — is, What would be gained by telling people my wife cheated on me?

By telling, you would attain the righteous position of being the vic-timized party. But assigning fault doesn't really change anything, and this disclosure might devastate others. Being the injured party isn't very satisfying for very long.

You do not owe it to your wife to protect her from her own behav-ior, nor do you owe anyone an explanation for what is essentially a private decision. You can say, "We put up a good front, but we feel it's best for both of us if we split." Make sure your kids know that they are loved beyond measure, now and always.

Don't react out of anger. Take time to make the most ethical decision.

In-Laws

· · · · · · · · · · · · · · · · · · · ·

The Good, the Bad, the Obnoxious

In-laws ignore parents' boundaries

DEAR AMY: My husband and I have a very strict bath and bedtime schedule that we follow every night with our 11-month-old son. When dropping him off at his grandparents' for a sleepover recently, we went over his routine with them and explained how important this consistency is for him. They agreed to it.

The next morning we learned that not only did they not follow the routine (he didn't end up going to bed until two hours after his usual time), but when giving him his bath, my husband's mom was in the bathtub with him, nude.

This is not the first time she has overstepped her boundaries. In the past when we talked to her about boundaries, she got extremely upset and accused us of not appreciating anything she does for our family. How should I approach these important issues with her?

— *Mad Mom*

DEAR MAD: I believe in the importance of routine for babies and children, but your adherence to this strict schedule is more for you than your son, and you should realize this.

Here's what you know: Your in-laws will not respect your son's schedule when he is with them. My view is that time spent with grandparents should be looser than life at home. Your mother-in-law's choice to bathe nude with her grandson shows poor judgment, and I agree that this crosses the line (though she may have done this with her children at that age).

When you've talked to her about boundaries in the past, she has retaliated by accusing you of being unappreciative. Remove this red herring by expressing your appreciation. Make sure your in-laws provide a safe environment for your child. Encourage an attitude of open dialogue by asking their opinion (they've already raised children — you're just starting). You shouldn't do another overnight until you are more confident in their ability to respect your wishes.

Childbearing isn't in-laws' business

DEAR AMY: My son's wife has finally decided (after three years of try-ing to have a baby) that she just doesn't want to be a parent.

She refuses to adopt (she can't conceive), and my son is torn be-cause he does want a family. She now thinks their marriage is in jeop-ardy. Both are 32 and have been married for six years. My concern is we can't seem to get her to have a conversation about why she doesn't want to be a parent. Any advice you can share for two young adults?

— *Lost Grandpa*

DEAR GRANDPA: My first recommendation is for you. This is a highly painful, personal (and, for many people, private) topic. Your son is confiding in you, which is great, but your reaction to him should be circumspect.

"We" — meaning you, alongside your son (and possibly other fam-ily members) — should not be initiating conversations with your daughter-in-law about why she "doesn't want to be a parent." You should not pressure her to make a choice (or even discuss this if she doesn't want to).

This crisis should be mediated by someone who does not have a personal stake. Signing your letter "Lost Grandpa" tells me you are viewing this through the prism of what it means to you (being a grandparent). A family therapist with expertise in this extremely challenging issue will help your son and his wife.

You should continue to actively emotionally support your son and be a champion for their marriage. But you should not mediate this issue unless both the husband and the wife come to you and ask for your input.

Volatile child creates family drama

DEAR AMY: My husband and our two children spend time with his sister and her children. One of her children inevitably hits one of our children at least a couple of times during each visit. Sometimes the parents will discipline him.

I have told my daughter that if this boy hits her, she should tell an adult (namely, the boy's parents), but time and again they do nothing about it. Sometimes they even try to suggest that my daughter is lying when she reports she has been hit.

This boy has quite a few behavior issues and should not be playing unsupervised with the other children, but his parents don't supervise him. I don't like to penalize my daughter by forcing her to remain under constant supervision for her own safety.

Is there ever a point where it is OK to tell her that if this child hits her that she can hit him back? I fear that this is the only way he will learn to stop hitting her.

— *Annoyed Mom*

DEAR MOM: You should never instruct your daughter to hit someone. I understand your logic, but if this boy can't control his impulses, then your daughter's retaliation could bring on nothing more productive than a backyard brawl.

You should instruct your daughter to tell this boy, "No hitting!" and to leave the area (and tell an adult) if he does. Children usually have an instinct to stay away from a volatile child. You should encourage your daughter to listen to her own instincts in this regard and stay well away from this cousin.

In-law's tradition is a burning issue

DEAR AMY: My mother-in-law alternates Christmas holidays with our family and my husband's two siblings. She is generally a well-behaved guest, but brings one tradition I can no longer tolerate. She burns a bayberry candle each Christmas Eve, believing this will guarantee her prosperity in the coming year.

Once it is lit, she insists that the candle burn completely or her fortune will be derailed. This is not a jar candle, but a candle stick. We attend church on Christmas Eve as our special tradition and for obvious reasons, I am not comfortable leaving my home with an unattended flame.

She created such a fuss this year that my husband allowed her to do it. I was furious at the thought of her ignorance in putting our home, contents and family pets at risk for her own self-interest. The incident ruined my entire Christmas Eve and quite frankly affected my enjoyment of her entire visit.

I think it is important to always honor and respect the rules of the host and hostess. How do I say no to this dangerous tradition?

— *Flamed in Ohio*

DEAR FLAMED: I agree with you that it is risky to keep a candle burning in an empty house, though there might be ways to reduce (if not eliminate) the risk. For instance, she could use a different kind of candle, which you could set in the fireplace (if you have one). She could also offer to stay home during church to guard her tradition — and your home.

Also, Christmas Eve lasts 24 hours. Perhaps she could burn the candle during the day, before you leave the house.

You and your husband should survey his other siblings to see how they deal with this. Then they should provide a united front in advising their mother of how dangerous this is and helping her find a safer way to enjoy this tradition.

I want less, and more, from my in-laws

DEAR AMY: My husband and I work full-time jobs six days a week. My in-laws watch our children one day a week. My problem is that whenever my husband and I have a day off to finally relax together as a family, my in-laws will call to ask us to dinner or see what our plans are. I value the little bit of family time we have with our children, so I don't feel like going out to dinner with my in-laws (it's not fun with two toddlers).

My husband and I disagree. He thinks I don't like his parents, particularly his mother. That's not true. His parents are very nice people, but I am a private person, and I do not think it's necessary for them to know how much money we make, how much all of our bills are and what we pay for anything we buy (we are in good shape financially, but I feel it's nobody's business). Also, his mother calls him just about every day and acts like her 37-year-old son is 15.

I don't understand why we have to accommodate them all of the time. In fact, it would be nice if they would offer to watch the children one night so my husband and I could go out to dinner ourselves. I feel it is my husband's obligation to have them back off, but he thinks I'm being an antisocial brat. I think I deserve to be a little selfish when it comes to spending time with my family.

— *Irritated in Idaho*

DEAR IRRITATED: You seem fine with your in-laws' willingness to take care of the kids, and while I agree that spending time with them on your one free night is too much to do, every week, you counter their expectation by expecting them to offer additional child care for you.

Your gripe might better be directed toward your husband, who you claim is indiscreet concerning your personal business. I agree that this is a problem. You will both have to establish boundaries with your in-laws, but you can't remove yourself completely from their orbit, and he won't establish these boundaries with them because he doesn't think it's a problem.

Help each other find a compromise. He might have dinner with his folks one night most weeks (he is their primary interest), enabling you to spend time with all of them less often.

Mother-in-law grosses out relatives

DEAR AMY: My husband and I have been happily married for two years. His family has welcomed me with open arms, and I am grateful for their kindness and enjoy their company. The problem is my mother-in-law's cooking. She does not wash her hands! I have caught her putting her fingers in food, licking her fingers and putting her fingers back in the same dish.

During our Christmas visit, she and I went grocery shopping. We returned and prepared the leftovers. She "re-mashed" the potatoes with her bare hands — without ever washing her hands! Amy, my husband and I are disgusted. Is there any way to bring this to her attention without hurting her feelings?

— *Grossed Out*

DEAR GROSSED OUT: This is extremely unappetizing, not to mention unhealthy. If your mother-in-law handled uncooked chicken or shellfish and then plunged her unwashed hands directly into a bowl of mashed potatoes, for instance, this could cross-contaminate foods and spread food-borne illness.

If you were pregnant and contracted listeria from these unsanitary practices, it could be disastrous. The Centers for Disease Control offers recommendations for safe food handling practices — and washing utensils and hands is paramount (check cdc.gov).

Because your husband was presumably raised by his mother and is also grossed out by this, one wonders if she has always done this — or if this is a new development. If it's new, his mother could have her own health issues leading to this behavior.

Bringing this up shouldn't cause conflict, though your mother-in-law might be a little stung. Try saying: "Mom, I'm very concerned about hand washing in the kitchen and I notice you're pretty casual about it. Can you help me out here? I feel like I can't eat comfortably unless the cook washes her hands often."

Financial advisor should be presented as bridal gift

DEAR AMY: I do not want to attend my future daughter-in-law's bridal shower. She and my stepson have lived together for more than two years and have a son together. I do many things for this grandson. I do not want him to suffer because of his parents' poor judgment.

After Christmas, I spent more than $300 on clothes for the little guy because the mother lamented that he needed them. They had used gift cards we gave them to make purchases for themselves. They live on my stepson's small salary and credit cards.

We are giving them $10,000 plus the rehearsal dinner for 60 people and the bar bill at the reception for 250 to 300 people. I feel once you have lived together and have a child together, you don't have a formal wedding with the white dress, 16 bridal attendants, destination bachelor and bachelorette parties, a 10-day honeymoon, etc. Especially when you are in debt.

After we told the bride what we would contribute, she said that my husband and I should probably take out a loan so we could do more for the wedding. I would like to send a modest gift and my regrets. Is that OK?

— Disappointed

DEAR DISAPPOINTED: You can do whatever you want to do. However, if you don't attend this event, your relationship with this couple — such as it is — will be affected. If you don't go to the shower, then it is not necessary to send a gift.

You and your husband should establish exactly whatever financial boundaries you choose, and stick with your promises, regardless of the pressure this couple exerts. The best gift to them might be a session with a financial adviser. Their debt load will bury them, and if you and your husband are not willing to bail them out, you should make this clear and stick to your guns.

Parents say 'no' to foreclosed family

DEAR AMY: My daughter and son-in-law are losing their house to foreclosure. We are not very fond of our son-in-law. He hasn't worked much in the last two years. He has a business that he continues to run that is losing money every month. He is also a sexual offender and is awaiting trial for a sexual assault case. He has treated our daughter terribly for a long time, but she has forgiven him over and over again.

They now want to move in with us, and we have said no. We said our daughter and the kids can live with us, but we won't have him here. Our daughter says we are making her choose between him and us, but we say we just don't want him in our house. Our daughter is shocked that we have said no to her.

She thinks that we should do anything for her; she says she would do this if it were her child. Does our daughter have a right to move in with us, just because she is our child?

— Miffed Parents

DEAR MIFFED: You haven't said no to your daughter. You have said no to her husband, who according to you is a dangerous character. If he is what you say he is, you should ask that he keep his distance.

You have been very clear about the conditions under which you would consider this arrangement, and your daughter can either accept or reject the deal you're offering. It is your home and your life, and you can certainly dictate whom you intend to share it with. Rather than focusing on her entitlements as a daughter, she should start to think about her responsibilities as a mother.

If her husband is the monster you claim he is, then everyone in the family should be working toward one goal: to get their children into a safe, secure and stable environment.

Son-in-law's chewing habits turn off parents

DEAR AMY: Our son-in-law is intelligent and witty, but for some reason he chews noisily with his mouth open and talks with his mouth full.

We put up with it when dining with him (we only see him and his family a couple of times a year because they live across the country), but I'm concerned that these habits will keep him from advancing in his career as he should and also be harmful during luncheon job interviews.

Do you have any ideas on how to get this concern across to him without alienating him? Or should I just keep my mouth shut?

— *Concerned Mother-in-law*

DEAR CONCERNED: You should keep your mouth shut. And so should he.

Distant in-laws bridging the gap by moving close

DEAR AMY: My husband's parents live in a different state and we see them infrequently, which my husband and I feel is enough. He is not close to them, and we do not look forward to our visits. My mother-in-law is manipulative and seems to view her time with us as an opportunity to educate us on how to live our lives. My father-in-law just checks out.

In the past when my husband confronted her about this, my mother-in-law ended up in tears. As a result, for the past few years we have just been quietly biding our time during our visits and have basically stopped questioning their "advice" while in their presence. Given the infrequent visits, this approach has been tolerable.

However, now my in-laws have informed us they are planning to move to our area. This was a bombshell. We were the last people they told. We feel violated and angry. We are horrified at the idea of their inserting themselves into our lives this way.

Do we have the right to ask them not to move here? If not, how do we convey our need for space and limited contact with them? We understand that they may be hurt, but for our sake, we must set some boundaries.

— *Upset*

DEAR UPSET: You do not have the right to tell your in-laws where to live. You must, however, be honest with them about how this affects you. I agree with you that it is vital that you do your best to establish boundaries with them. Nodding in agreement while you wait for your encounters with them to end will no longer work.

Your husband should take the lead here and steel himself for tears and manipulation. He should be calm, kind, resolute and realize that his parents are adults and are responsible for their own choices.

In-laws want too much — a kidney

DEAR AMY: One of my in-laws needs a new kidney. She will be undergoing the transplant process soon.

Her family wanted me to give her one of my kidneys. My family said no to this, and so I did not get tested beyond the blood test (we are the same blood group). Now my in-laws are angry and have stopped talking to me. I would like to know how my sick relative is doing, but I don't know what to say when I call — or whether I should call.

In the past they have said horrible things to me because I did not donate my kidney; it seems now that our long friendship is meaningless. I still care for her and her family, but how do I let them know that I am thinking about them? I know if I try to call, the woman who is getting the transplant will say nasty things to me. What should I do?

— *Upset*

DEAR UPSET: If donating an organ is what it takes to get in good with your in-laws, then their standards are a tad unreasonable. I assume there are other dynamics at play which created this pressure on you, but if you are eager to reach this in-law but don't want to risk the verbal backlash, then the best way to do so is through a greeting card.

When you send a message through the mail, you lessen the opportunity for back talk.

Christmas Eve gift brings on question

DEAR AMY: I enjoy a wonderful relationship with my in-laws, and this Christmas Eve is the first one when they will be celebrating with my parents at our home. Our tradition is that the kids are permitted to open one gift from each grandparent on Christmas Eve. My mother-in-law bought my son a video gaming system along with a ton of 3-D games for his present. They are considerably more well-off than my family, and I am afraid that my parents will feel upstaged. How do I handle this without hurting feelings or making things awkward?

— *Santa's Helper*

DEAR HELPER: Aside from the upstaging issue, this gift is simply too much to be given on Christmas Eve. If the boy is permitted to open it, he will naturally want to play with it. Given the setup time and obsessive nature of these games, if he receives them on Christmas Eve, he will be unable to see straight the next day.

Though I like the tradition of receiving a gift on Christmas Eve, it is important to keep it modest. Explain to your in-laws that the tradition is for the kids to open one small and simple gift (a book, for instance).

Toxic in-law gives the turkey a bad taste

DEAR AMY: I've been married 29 years to a great guy, and we have two grown sons who are terrific. My husband's sister is a meddler and complainer — and we are her target.

She has (many times) called our sons and told them, "Your mother is doing this and that wrong," and the kids ignore her, but they are upset afterward. I've told my husband to tell her to knock it off. He refuses, so I nicely told her that her complaining was inappropriate. I asked her to stop behaving this way around us. She said, "It's your problem."

Now my husband wants her to join us for Thanksgiving (for the first time). We have a really nice group of 14 people who join us annually. I am saying "no way" — she meddles, trash talks, and complains. (His mother, long gone, would say, "Don't invite her!")

Here are our choices: Thanksgiving for five, with none of our usual group; or Thanksgiving for 15, and I guarantee several won't come the following year. I don't want her to hold us hostage. I also don't want her in our home. She has other good Thanksgiving options. I'm pretty firm (and nice) with my "no way," but my husband is trying to get me to relent. He admits that he doesn't want her to come but she is insisting.

Other than inviting her, what do you suggest?

— *Not Thankful*

DEAR NOT: Maybe it's me — but isn't it a little early in the year to worry about Thanksgiving? And do you have a history of relenting to repeated queries, or doesn't your husband know the meaning of "no means no"?

Because he seems powerless at the hands of his toxic sister, you might relieve him of this burden by saying that the next time his sister asks about Thanksgiving, he can just have her give you a call.

Mom-in-law's email not so innocent

DEAR AMY: Years ago, after one of my husband's co-workers began to forward pornographic emails to my husband, we had a discussion about pornography and pictures of naked women. Because it bothers me, my husband asked his friend to stop these emails, which he did.

My mother-in-law is one of those people constantly forwards "junk" emails to my husband, as well as to tons of other people. She recently forwarded an email containing motorcycle pictures. Each of the motorcycles had a naked woman next to it.

When we told my mother-in-law that this was a completely inappropriate email to send to my husband, she claimed that she hadn't even thought about the fact that it contained naked women, she just thought that my husband would like to see the motorcycles.

However, as I pointed out, she had only sent it to my husband and his uncle. Usually her forwards go out to tons of people. And as I pointed out, she hadn't sent it to her son-in-law, which tells me that she respects her daughter's marriage but not mine.

I find her behavior and the fact that she is claiming it was an innocent email (if it was so innocent, then why didn't she email it to more people?) despicable and disrespectful of me and my marriage. What are your thoughts on this?

— *Furious Wife*

DEAR WIFE: My reaction is that your mother-in-law has really figured out how to get your goat. This email was sent to your husband (not to you). You have most likely correctly identified what she is doing and why. Your husband has bowed to your sensitivities in the past by successfully drawing a boundary. He should do so again. The less involvement and personal reaction you have, the better.

Mother-in-law's baking isn't enough with a bun in the oven

DEAR AMY: My mother-in-law is a fantastic baker. The best. However, her idea of breakfast when we visit is muffins and juice. My idea of breakfast is a pretty substantial cereal with muffins (or cinnamon rolls or scones or her other specialty of the day) as a side. There's no way I can eat just a pastry for breakfast and make it through the morning.

Is it rude for me to bring milk and cereal into their house for breakfast when we are visiting for a few days? I feel as if I can get away with it now because I'm pregnant, but in the future don't know how to handle this.

— *Expectant Daughter-in-law*

DEAR EXPECTANT: You should give your mother-in-law the opportunity to beef up her breakfast offerings before bringing groceries into her home.

In advance of your next visit, say to her, "I'm on a breakfast routine and usually eat (name the brand) cereal. I absolutely love your baked goods, but would be OK if we also had some cereal in the morning? I'd be happy to bring it along with us when we come." Good hosts (and she is definitely one) enjoy making their guests feel at home. Give her a chance to do this for you.

Work

. . . .

It's Not Work If You Love It — but First You Have to Find It

First job eludes new college grad

DEAR AMY: I'm 23 and recently graduated from college. After I moved back home, I realized that there aren't any available jobs in my field of study. I have no job experience, no car (or license), and my student loans bills are starting to pile up.

I've been struggling to find a job for months. However, no one seems to be willing to hire me because of my lack of work experience. I don't want to be a burden on my family. Any advice?

— *Worried*

DEAR WORRIED: Volunteer for an organization whose goals you share. Take any paying gigs you can get, including baby-sitting, plant-watering, cleaning houses or shoveling snow. Work on getting a driver's license (even if you don't have access to a car, this skill is important).

Everybody has a first job — eventually. Any experience (paid or volunteer) will help your pitch, keep you busy, and bring in dough while you continue to pursue your first professional opportunity.

Driving skill important, even without car

DEAR AMY: I really don't like to drive, and owning a car seems to be more trouble than it's worth. My parents say I can't get a job unless I learn to drive. Can you give me some advice about how to handle this?

— *Lousy Driver*

DEAR LOUSY: One way to handle this is to become a less lousy driver. The less lousy you are, the more confident you will be, the more enjoyable you will find this skill, and the safer you (and others) will be on the road. The ability to safely operate a vehicle is important, even if you decide that ultimately you don't want to own a car or drive regularly. If you are able to drive, it will increase your employment options; it also means you would be able to drive someone (or yourself) in an emergency. Driving will also put you in good stead in the event that we all find ourselves in some sort of apocalyptic "Mad Max" future.

Job seekers should mind their grammar

DEAR AMY: My partner and I run a small business and are in the process of hiring employees. We have asked candidates to fill out an application and to send us their resumes via e-mail. The errors on the applications are astonishing: incomplete sentences, numerous spelling errors, format inconsistencies, and an absence of periods and capitalization.

Most of our applicants are recent college graduates. While perfect grammar is not a requirement of this position, attention to detail is important. We want to say something to our applicants to encourage them to take more time on future job applications. Making a good first impression is important. However, we aren't sure that this is our place. If we speak up, how should we approach the topic in a professional, nonthreatening way?

— Conflicted

DEAR CONFLICTED: It is not your duty to educate these rookie applicants, but you would be doing them a favor — as well as conveying your company's expectations and image — by attaching simple instructions before you invite them to apply.

Your letter should say something like, "We look forward to learning more about you. Keep in mind, however, that the application is your first opportunity to impress us. Please use special care with your writing, spelling, grammar and format. Those applications that don't conform to a basic standard will not make it past the first cut."

Work tension leaves reader baffled

DEAR AMY: I work at an assisted living facility. There is one co-worker I find hard to deal with. She bosses people around and interferes with job assignments. She is rude and disrespectful, as well.

I went to the nursing supervisor because her behavior was affecting the residents. The co-worker stopped for a while, but now she is starting again. This situation is causing me a lot of stress.

— Nursed Out

DEAR NURSED: Your supervisor has intervened once, and it seemed to have an effect on your co-worker's behavior.

Go back to your supervisor. Say the problem has surfaced again. This time, however, ask for suggestions.

Your particular professional challenge is to not only serve people in an intimate way who have a variety of personalities and abilities, but also to work cooperatively with people who have varied temperaments.

You may be able to change the dynamic if you react differently when your co-worker attempts to dominate you. Telling her, "Thank you, but I already know my assignments for today," is a respectful but fairly definitive way to ask her to back off.

You should be open to other ideas.

Child laborer fed up with parents

DEAR AMY: I'm a 12-year-old girl with three older siblings, ages 14, 16, and 17. My parents make us clean the house every weekend. Every time we're done, my mom or dad will yell about how we didn't do the job right.

I love my parents to death, and they give me a lot, but this is getting tiring. It feels as if they're never happy with the work we do. It doesn't matter if it takes me 30 minutes or two hours — they're still not happy. I try to tell them I'm trying my best, but they just yell. I've been cleaning my house since I was 7 or 8 because, being the youngest, I started earlier than my siblings.

I want to ask you what's the best way to approach my parents without their yelling at me and saying I'm lying. I feel they see me as a maid sometimes, and I don't know what to do. Is it just me being lazy, or is it my parents — or both?

— *Tired*

DEAR TIRED: I'm hardly impartial because I am a parent, and while I seldom raise my voice, my daughter once told me that I "yelled with my eyes." I'm also a former kid who, at your age, was working with my siblings toting milk pails each night on our dairy farm.

I remember the discouraged feeling you describe when you feel nothing you do is "right." When you are older, you'll look back on your childhood labor and in all likelihood be very happy that you worked at home, but for now it might ease your frustration if you asked your parents to write down a "chore chart," breaking down your cleaning duties.

On the chart they can list step-by-step instructions and goals. As you go through your chores, you can check off each of these as you finish. For instance: "Laundry: Remove clothes from dryer, sort, fold and put away."

Nothing bugs parents more than a job they consider "half-done." Communicate with your folks about what exactly constitutes a finished job, and ask them to recognize it when you do it well. Sometimes we parents are so busy yelling with our eyes that we forget to say "thank you!"

Prospective employer 'went in another direction'

DEAR AMY: Last week I interviewed for a job opening in a different department at my company. The two-hour interview went great; we have similar goals and had worked together in the past. Two days after the interview, I received a four-sentence email, copying the interviewer's boss and our HR manager, informing me that I did not get the job. She wrote that she "went in another direction."

I was shocked. I immediately sent an email back thanking her for the opportunity and asking for suggestions on what I could've done better or what training would be helpful — basically I was asking for feedback of any sort.

I haven't heard back, of course. After I sent the email, I broke down in tears. Last month I also applied for an in-house position. My interviewers told me in person that I wasn't selected and offered to help me with other opportunities. I felt respected, appreciated and valued, even though I didn't get the job.

Is email an accepted way to tell someone she hasn't been selected?

— *Appalled Baby Boomer*

DEAR APPALLED: Email is acceptable for this purpose. It creates a record of the interchange, for one thing, and the phrase "We went in another direction" is code for just about anything. I agree with you that this seems cowardly, especially within your own company, but I reflect to my own experience.

I interviewed extensively for a job and then when I hadn't heard anything for more than a week, I called the person who interviewed me and he replied, "Oh — yeah. I hired a guy younger than you. He went to Harvard. You know how it is. He started yesterday. Sorry, I guess I should have told you."

Boy, I wish I'd had that one in writing.

Negativity is infectious

DEAR AMY: I'm a teacher and have five work friends with whom I like to do things.

One of these friends, however, is driving me insane. She's a conversation hijacker who will take over any conversation with tales of herself. These stories are generally laments about the school, her health and her work partner. It's awful, negative and makes me not want to gather with the other four ladies, whom I like. I've virtually stopped going to lunch so as to avoid going crazy.

How can I get her to stop without totally offending her?

— *Taxed Teacher*

DEAR TAXED: You can convey your reaction tactfully and truthfully, and your colleague can either take your statement in the spirit it's offered — or add it to her list of lamentations.

So you can say, "You know how they say enthusiasm is infectious? Well, so is negativity. We don't have much time for lunch, and when we go out you spend a lot of time on your own stuff when I really want to visit with everyone."

Co-worker dates cheater

DEAR AMY: I am a 23-year-old woman. Recently, I found out that one of my co-workers is going out with a guy I dated during two separate periods. He cheated on me both times.

I am friends with this co-worker outside of work and felt it was best to tell her about his cheating. She confronted him about the cheating, and he denied it, of course. She now insists on staying with him, and it's killing me. He doesn't deserve to be happy. Is it abnormal to still feel bitter toward him?

— Jackie

DEAR JACKIE: It is not abnormal to feel bitter toward someone who cheated on you. Don't let the bitterness take over, though — because then the bad guy wins. Cheaters aren't happy — at least not for long. Cheaters are chasing happiness, and they never find it for long.

Passion is elusive for this young worker

DEAR AMY: I am single, in my middle 20s and have a good job. This job pays well, and I could potentially have this job for the rest of my career. I am liked by my colleagues, and my supervisor has assured me that my job is secure.

That being said, I do not feel as though I am fulfilling my passion in this job. I could work here for the next 30 years and be financially well off. I do not, however, know what my passion is or what I would do if I left this job.

In this economy, it is easy to justify staying in a job a person is not especially happy with. I know that jobs are difficult to get now and a person should be thankful to have one at all.

What are your thoughts, Amy? How does a person find a passion? Is it a good idea to leave a secure job to seek the unknown, with the hopes of finding a passion?

— Wondering

DEAR WONDERING: Passion can be elusive. The more energetically you chase it, the faster it skittles away. But chasing passion will lead you in unexpected directions. The search will lead to people, experiences, discovery and insight.

You shouldn't leave your job right now. Nor should you consider your job to be a pair of golden handcuffs, shackling you to an uninspiring career for the next three decades. Take a look around your workplace. Are there functions outside of your area you would like to try? Does your workplace offer seminars, training opportunities, fellowships or opportunities to learn about and perhaps work in other divisions?

In your time outside of work, you should read, travel, volunteer, listen to music, go to art openings and theater performances. Take up fencing or knitting. Develop some interests and expertise outside your work life, and your passion may find you.

'Career girl' should act like grown-up

DEAR AMY: I am a 26-year-old "career girl" who works on a team that consists of all men in their 40s and 50s. These gentlemen have always treated me with respect. It is obvious that they value the job that I do at our company.

Recently a new team member was brought on who is also a personal friend of my boss's. This new team member, "Jon," does not treat me as a professional equal. Instead Jon gives me his busy work, talks down to me and is generally disrespectful.

I feel that his pride has made it difficult for him to work with me because of my status at our company, the fact that I'm younger than he is, the fact that I'm a woman or maybe a combination of all three. I'm only a little bit older than his daughters.

How do I express to Jon that I am not his personal assistant? Because this person is also a friend of the boss's, should I involve my superior or try to handle this on my own? I don't want to seem like a tattletale, but I'm harboring a lot of resentment, and I know it will only get worse if I don't confront the issue.

— *Workplace Woes*

DEAR WORKPLACE: You could start by never, ever, in any context, referring to yourself as a "career girl." Even reading that phrase makes me want to send you out for coffee.

Your colleague can't just "give" you busy work. He can attempt to assign a task to you, but if this task isn't in your job description and if he is a recent hire, then you will have to educate him. Say, "I'm sorry, 'Jon,' but I'm going to toss this back to you. I don't handle administrative tasks for other team members."

You might be contributing to this dynamic by acting like an ingénue (you certainly write like one). So unless you are auditioning for an episode of "Mad Men," then stop it. Don't make assumptions about why your colleague is behaving badly — but respond to the behavior quickly, appropriately and professionally.

As the new guy, if he has a problem with you, then he can go whine to the boss.

Lack of greeting drives airline worker crazy

DEAR AMY: I work at an airline ticket counter and have kiosks in front of me where people check themselves in. Many times a passenger will simply start talking to me without any type of greeting. No "excuse me" or "hello."

This drives me crazy. Would someone do this to people in a grocery store, on the street? I have said many times in the past, "Good morning!" only to hear them repeat what they said to me the first time. Yes, some passengers then say, "I'm sorry, good morning," or, "How are you?" What would you recommend in instances like this? I think it's very rude.

— *The Last Straw*

DEAR LAST: I understand your frustration, and I agree that speaking to someone without greeting her first is rude.

If you make eye contact and interrupt by saying, "Hello. How are you?" this will often shock a person into politeness. But please remember that you have all the power. Travelers in airports are sometimes freaked-out, quivering blobs of lateness (or maybe that's just me).

'Work wife' thinks she's hot stuff

DEAR AMY: I've worked in an office with all men for more than 10 years. They are all married, but I've always been like the "work wife." Over the past several years, one of the men and I have become especially close friends. He and his wife basically just live together. They are married in name only.

Recently, we have progressed from harmless flirting to an affair. We are very careful not to let anyone know, especially at work. I have no expectations of him leaving his wife due to their financial/family situation.

Meanwhile, I've met a fabulous single guy whom I enjoy spending time with, but I only see him a couple of times a month. He's about ready to retire and is trying to save as much money as he can. There is a possible long-term future with him. My problem is the feelings I have for my co-worker are so strong. We share an unbelievable connection. I want to continue both relationships until I see where it all goes. I'm 50-plus years old and have never done this type of thing before.

Am I playing with fire? What should I do?

— *Fabulous at Fifty*

DEAR FABULOUS: If your behavior is what makes you fabulous, then I seriously need to rethink my own life. You express not a shred of guilt or sadness over your choices: the impact on the marriage that you are willingly, even happily, infringing upon — or the impact on your or this other person's careers. Is this fabulous? Decidedly not. You are, in fact, playing with fire. My advice is for you to stoke the embers in somebody else's barbecue pit.

Resume reviewer wants to help applicant

DEAR AMY: Part of my job is to review resumes. I will typically inform job seekers via email that their resume will be kept on file for future consideration. I recently received a resume that, while sincere (not spam), was atrocious. The grammar and vocabulary were awful, and the format was poor to the point of near-illegibility.

Despite this, the candidate stated that he had completed a bachelor's degree, had working experience and English oral presentation skills. I feel very strongly that he will never be hired if he continues to submit this resume, as is. How can I diplomatically suggest that he seek the advice of a career counselor, as well as additional lessons in written English? I don't want to give offense or be misunderstood.

— *Want to Help*

DEAR WANT TO HELP: You would be doing this person a service by responding, "Though my company won't be hiring you, I wanted to offer you some suggestions for improving your resume so that you can present your very best self to other potential employers."

There are many online sources for resume writing, send the person a link. You can also suggest that the job seeker do an Internet search on "career counseling" in his area. This seeker would be wise to follow your suggestions.

Close to retirement, communication breaks down

DEAR AMY: I am approaching full retirement age and have been working for the same organization for more than 35 years in a professional capacity. The department head has ceased to speak to me (I have worked with him for 25 years), and whenever he has a question, he asks my colleague to ask me. I feel bullied through non-communication, and I feel that he is pressuring me to leave sooner than I'd planned.

Either that, or he is no longer valuing my contribution. I have not confronted him with this issue because he will just deny it. I have a pleasant working relationship with my immediate manager and other colleagues. Should I just grin and bear it until I leave? I don't like confrontations. The current situation is affecting my health.

— *Feeling My Age*

DEAR FEELING: You have the best motive in the world (your health) to try to get to the bottom of this. You may not be able to effect much change at this point, but you will at least have expressed yourself. This is not a confrontation but gathering information that affects you.

Tell your immediate manager the chain of communication seems to be broken, and ask him or her if there are any issues you need to be aware of.

You might be advised to contact the department head directly. If so, pose your query neutrally and accept the answer — even if there is none. If he denies there is a problem, then all the better — take his word for it and move on.

Payroll clerk questions payroll padding

DEAR AMY: I work for a small company and the hourly staff is on the honor system when it comes to filling out their time sheets. I do the payroll. One employee is overstating her hours to get overtime benefits.

I brought this up to the controller who basically said, "If that's what she wrote, then that's what we'll pay her." The employee in question has worked for the company for over 15 years.

I don't want the woman fired, but at least question her, give her a warning or better yet, install a time clock. Should I go over the controller's head and let the owner know that this employee is basically stealing from the company?

— *Concerned Employee*

DEAR CONCERNED: Because you handle the payroll and have already brought this to the controller's attention, you could follow up with an email.

Say, "Based on the concerns I raised with you the other day, I suggest we install a time clock to ensure that all employees accurately report their hours."

You are suggesting a change in the way you do things, so you should copy the company owner on this email, alerting him or her to the issue.

The owner can then follow up with the controller and make a decision about what to do.

Can romance grow in cubicle farm?

DEAR AMY: I have recently been spending more time with a new co-worker. The more I get to know her, the more interested I become.

We are both unattached and have made your column our morning routine when we work together. We both have had previous bad experiences in relationships. Now I'm having a hard time not asking her out for a date. She wants to be single, and I can understand her feelings about putting her career first.

I think she knows I want more, yet I'm reluctant to make any move that would ruin the friendship we have begun. I'm usually good at giving advice on these matters, but I could really use an outsider's opinion. I don't know what to do.

— *Interested Friend*

DEAR INTERESTED: Thank you for making my column part of your workday routine. Judging from the mail I receive from worker bees, this column serves as conversation fodder in many cubicle farms.

Your co-worker seems to be telegraphing that she will not be receptive to a romance with you. All the same, I know the irrepressible impulse of wanting to ask someone out.

I say: Relieve the pressure by bringing this up, but anticipate being kindly refused. Here's how you can do it: "Amy seems to think I should ask you to do something outside of work. I'm not sure. What do you think?"

Tweeted ire leads to employee fire

DEAR AMY: This week I was fired from a customer service job. The incident leading to my firing happened when I was exhausted and caught off guard by a very young customer who was angry with an answer I gave her. I was not at my best but tried to steer her to my manager. The girl refused to see the manager and tweeted about me and my company that night. The next day I called my supervisor to alert her about the angry customer. I was totally shocked to hear that our headquarters had caught wind of the angry tweet, which stated that I was unkind to this customer.

I am a compassionate person and about three times as old as this customer (she is probably about 20). Please tell your readers to count to 10 when they are angry, even if they are "right" in a commercial situation. It is a test of character to know how to complain about people.

— *Fired*

DEAR FIRED: Twitter and Facebook (and other social networking sites) have made it very easy for consumers to tweet their praise about products and services. These same tools are being used by consumers to complain about services and single out specific employees.

I admit to having done this myself. Recently, after a frustrating encounter with an airline employee during a delayed flight, I took to Twitter with a nonspecific, snarky complaint, neatly delivered in 140 characters.

Within minutes, I heard back from the corporate office of the airline, asking for the name of the employee I was complaining about. I declined to provide it. Sometimes a complaint is a vent — and not grounds for punishment or dismissal.

I agree with your admonition to count to 10 before pressing "send" and urge companies not to overreact to unverified tweets or postings, especially when these complaints could be used to improve service through training.

Boundaries

Drawing, Building and Reinforcing

Something's fishy about therapist

DEAR AMY: For 18 months, my wife has had therapy with a professional psychologist. Though this woman has definitely been helpful, I question her ethics. When we traveled to another part of the country last fall, the psychologist told my wife, "You know, I do accept gifts."

Then she went on to mention her favorite packaged fish from the area we were visiting. Despite my reluctance, my wife brought this back for her. Yesterday, the psychologist asked my wife (who is a musician) if she wouldn't mind performing at her nephew's birthday party. This is a family affair at an expensive restaurant, and the psychologist suggested that my wife and I were "welcome" to get our own table.

Though none of this bothers my easygoing wife, I feel her psychologist is stepping over the boundaries of ethical behavior. What's your take?

— *The Questioning Husband*

DEAR HUSBAND: Your wife's therapist has not only stepped over ethical boundaries, she has vaulted over them. Your wife is paying the therapist for therapy. This exchange should not extend beyond the therapist's office. And though a relationship between the two is inevitable (and positive), your easygoing wife should realize that her therapist is manipulating and taking advantage of her.

Even if your wife doesn't mind this breach, this will inevitably interfere with the therapeutic work the two are supposed to do together. It is the therapist's job to recognize and adhere to her professional ethical standards, not to burden her client with the issue of wondering how to enforce boundaries and manage the relationship.

Your wife should decline this musical gig. She should also discuss this issue in therapy — and look for another therapist. The American Psychological Association has posted ethical guidelines on its website, apa.org.

Lakefront runner worries about greeting

DEAR AMY: I was running on the lakefront path early this morning. I passed two runners who were missing one leg each and were wearing prosthetics.

I have the utmost respect for any runner, but especially for someone who is disabled. As I passed by them, I smiled and said, "You're both amazing!" Neither of them looked happy to receive this compliment, and I almost think they looked a little annoyed.

The rest of my run I was wondering if I offended them and thought maybe they didn't like being called out. I know my intentions were good, but I still feel bad if I offended them. Do you think it's better to not say anything next time I'm in a similar situation?

— *Runner*

DEAR RUNNER: You meant well and should not worry too much about this, but surely you can imagine that having an obvious disability subjects these runners to frequent comments, and that sometimes they might simply like to run along the path just like everyone else.

Unless you pass a group of young children whose running you feel compelled to encourage, then, yes, I do think it's better to treat all of your fellow runners as simply fellow athletes who are all more or less equally amazing.

Idling minivan irritates neighbor

DEAR AMY: My neighbor has three kids and a minivan. I work at home, and often notice she warms her car up for a long time (often 10 minutes or more) from a remote starter. She is polluting the air we all breathe unnecessarily and wasting gas.

I feel like she is infringing on my rights to live in a clean world where we already have such a climate crisis. Is there a way to address this with her?

— *Fretting in Oak Park*

DEAR FRETTING: By all means, advocate for the climate, but you could probably make the biggest impact by taking these kids to school in your pedicab. I assume you'll offer.

If you want to open up a conversation about carbon footprints, be aware that there are real and relational consequences. If you weigh in on your neighbor's polluting habits, she might decide she'd like to come to your house and evaluate your pollution-emitting carpet, furnace or roof shingles.

If you feel your health is at risk from your neighbor's vehicle exhaust, you have a right to ask her not to idle her van near your house. Know, however, that while you have the right to make any request you like, unless your neighbor is breaking a local statute or law, you cannot prevent her from doing as she pleases, including "wasting gas."

Young adult can't hold her liquor

DEAR AMY: My spouse and I recently attended a party at a friend's house. The hostess had her 20-year-old daughter stationed behind the bar to serve drinks. I thought it was nice that the daughter was willing to help out by serving guests.

However, the daughter also had set up a tip jar on the bar. Every time she poured a drink for a guest, she pointed to the tip jar as if to encourage a donation. What do you make of this, Amy?

— Mrs. C

DEAR MRS. C: Most 20-year-olds can't hold their liquor. I also don't want them holding mine. Such immature displays are why 20-year-olds should not be posted behind — or in front of — the bar.

Non-drinking guests worry about serving alcohol

DEAR AMY: My husband and I do not drink for personal reasons but do not have anything against it. However, when we host a party for our colleagues and friends, I often feel bad that we don't serve wine or beer. I'm wondering if there is a polite way to tell our guests to feel free to bring their own beverages without sounding as if we want them to provide them.

We wouldn't mind buying wine or beer ourselves, but since we don't drink, we have no idea what would be considered fine wine or good beer. Any suggestions?

— *Eager Hosts*

DEAR HOSTS: You are not socially obligated to provide alcohol for your friends when you entertain. But because you are open to serving it in your home even though you don't drink (good for you), you should seek direction from your local wine shop. Any wine seller would be more than happy to give you ideas for what to serve with whatever meal you are preparing.

Guests often offer to bring something to a meal. If you are inviting someone and he or she asks, "Is there anything I can bring?" You can say, "A bottle of wine or your favorite beer would be great. Thank you."

It's hard to forgive and forget insult

DEAR AMY: How do you handle it when a "friend" insults you publicly? Recently, my friend and I were part of a group working together at church. When I showed enthusiasm for something that we were doing, she stated, "Little things please little minds."

I was quite embarrassed to have that comment made in this circle of people whom I enjoy and respect. My instinct is to withdraw and to be quiet so I won't be insulted again. Although I want to forgive and forget to preserve the "friendship," I don't want to be treated this way. How would you handle this situation?

— *Sensitive Friend*

DEAR SENSITIVE: Honestly, I'm more likely to be on the other side of this equation — and so as a lifetime loudmouth, I'll tell you what I would want a friend to do if I insulted her publicly. I often say in this space, "Friends tell each other the truth," and so the burden is on you if you want to repair your friendship and — importantly — preserve your self-esteem.

When this person made this unfortunate remark, it would have been best if you had been able to react in the moment with honesty and a touch of humor. "Well, now, that's not at all embarrassing!" you could have said.

I think it's likely that your church colleague didn't realize that this remark would sting you so much. After the fact, you should privately educate her about how her behavior affected you. She may deflect or diminish your reaction — but that's her problem. If she's smart, she'll cop to this thoughtless remark and allow you to thoroughly forgive her. And then you should.

Marrying woman charges guests for attendance

DEAR AMY: I know a woman through my church who has led a rather chaotic life, with several children from different men, etc. She met a man at our church, and they are getting married.

She mailed an invitation to me and my husband, and it never arrived — which isn't surprising because we have ongoing problems with our mail service. However, she was registered with an online wedding site where guests can RSVP, and I responded "yes." The bride insisted on sending a new invitation through the mail. This time we received it, and I was completely shocked that she had included a self-addressed, stamped envelope to send either a check or money order for the cost of our wedding meals to her in advance. She included the price. She had already requested gift cards to specific places for a wedding gift.

I usually give money as a wedding gift, as I would prefer a couple buy whatever they want for themselves, but the idea of also sending money to attend the wedding really puts me out. I know when my husband and I got married, times were tough and we had the wedding we could afford. We didn't ask in advance for people to pay to attend. I don't even feel comfortable going to this event, but can I politely get out of it if I've already said we would go?

— *Distressed Guest*

DEAR DISTRESSED: Some marrying couples mistakenly believe that they should be compensated by their guests for the cost of hosting their own reception. These couples expect this compensation to come through the value of the gifts they receive. This transforms a wedding into an exchange of goods and services. Your friend is taking this one step further and has turned her wedding into a profit-making venture.

I can understand why you would no longer want to attend the reception. Because you all met at church, you could support your friend's marriage by attending the religious ceremony but not the reception. Let her know that your plans have changed. If she asks why, you can tell her you didn't realize until now that there was a cost for the reception and that it doesn't fit your budget. In these garter-tightening times, I'm sure she'll understand.

Bridesmaid gives and gives — and should give some more

DEAR AMY: I've been asked to be a bridesmaid in a close friend's wedding this summer. I'm honored that she asked me to be a part of this occasion. The dilemma I am facing is whether I should get her and her soon-to-be husband a wedding gift.

I have already spent a small fortune on my plane ticket and I am expected to pay for my own accommodations, transportation and bridesmaid's dress. Is it offensive to simply get them a heartfelt card and a hug instead of a gift? I'm not poor, but I feel I've already spent a lot of money and time making sure I'm there for her. Is my presence a good enough present?

I have several other weddings to attend this summer, and between all these events (and gifts), my purse is feeling a little tight, but I don't want these friends to think I don't care about them.

— *Unsure Bridesmaid*

DEAR BRIDESMAID: Bridal attendants spend and sacrifice a great deal to participate in a wedding, and yet, unless the wedding couple has specifically asked you not to, a gift should also be given. Sometimes attendants join together to give the couple a group gift (traditionally the bride will also give you and the other bridesmaids a gift to thank you for "attending" to her).

I like the idea of a group gift because it spreads the cost, while bundling the affection.

Military brat's moving patterns inhibit friendship

DEAR AMY: I was a military brat growing up. Our family moved every two years. As soon as I graduated from high school I joined the Air Force, where I moved a lot again. When I was young, I made friends really easily. Now that I am older (I'm 48), I find myself much more guarded.

I don't want to make friends because I'm afraid I'll get close to people and they will leave. So basically my wife is my only friend. We have been married for 25 years.

I just started a new job and work with a lot of nice people, but I find myself pulling away from them. Do you have any suggestion how I can get over my phobia?

— *New Guy*

DEAR NEW: Your current behavior is a very understandable reaction to your life. You describe your current concern as being about other people (not you) leaving, but if you are no longer in the military and plan to stay put for the next several years (I'm assuming), keep in mind that you have time to develop, build and grow relationships.

Time is something you've never really had — because the uncertainty and frequency of your transitions put you into friendship overdrive. This is a valuable and positive survival instinct, but most friendships progress one cup of coffee and one conversation at a time. Can you (and your wife) start there?

You understand your own motivations. A professional counselor would help nudge you toward change.

Perfume's scent causes fellow diner to choke

DEAR AMY: I just returned from a regular lunch spot in town. It is a nice, casual and comfortable place that seats maybe 60 people. When I arrived I was seated two tables away from a woman who had doused herself in strong perfume.

I moved three tables away and it was no better. Finally I spotted an opening four tables from her and took it. I choked down my lunch quickly and left — sick from her smell. Should restaurant owners address this issue? Is it ever appropriate for a patron to approach the offender?

— Distressed Diner

DEAR DISTRESSED: The restaurant's job is to try to make all of the diners comfortable, and the establishment did this by letting you hopscotch from table to table. However, despite your best efforts, when you are navigating in the world you will occasionally encounter people who impede your enjoyment.

If your fellow diner asked you why you were choking — or changing your table — you could have said, "I seem to be allergic to your perfume." Otherwise, no, it is not appropriate to approach another patron and say, "Your scent makes me sick."

Should older adults sit on each other's laps?

DEAR AMY: My spouse and I want to know: Is it socially appropriate for two adults (married to each other and in their 50s and 60s) to sit on each other's laps in a gathering in a family member's home?

At a recent birthday party for a young family member, my spouse's stepmother decided to take a seat on her husband's lap while he was seated on a breakfast stool. Hands were held and placed on knees/thighs in a relatively innocent manner; there was no additional kissing, groping, etc.

My spouse and I disagree on whether or not this was acceptable behavior for adults. One of us thinks that it is a clear instance of a teenage-style "public display of affection," and the other thinks that it was not a big deal because the two people involved were married adults and that there were only family members and close friends present at the time. What is your opinion?

— *Touchy-Feely in Chicago*

DEAR TOUCHY-FEELY: In a casual setting at a family member's home, I think it's fine — sweet, really. But is it "socially appropriate"? No. It's also potentially chair-breaking behavior. However, you ask about the propriety of these two older people sitting "on each other's laps." The man taking his turn sitting on the woman's lap makes this much more interesting. I'm all for it.

Gift cards create opportunity for generosity

DEAR AMY: When my husband and I have a restaurant gift card and go to dinner with another couple, we always offer to share the savings. We deduct the gift card amount from the entire bill and then split whatever is left. One of the couples we dine with, however, splits the bill and then uses their gift card to pay only for their portion of the bill.

Which is the correct way to do it?

— *L.F. in N.J.*

DEAR L.F.: Your way is the generous and polite way. I like the idea of spreading the savings to the group. Everybody wins! Using a gift card as "cash" to be used for your own dinner, however, is the more common way to handle this — at least that's my impression from the people who write in to me with questions about gift cards.

Widower ready to socialize, but how?

DEAR AMY: My wife passed away less than a year ago. We were married for almost seven years, and even though we had our hard times, we were really in love. My problem is that maybe we were too in love! We had a lot of friends but rarely did things with them. This was for different reasons (kids, jobs, etc.).

The problem I'm having now is finding something to do where I don't either invite myself or feel like a third wheel. The last thing I want is for people to feel sorry for me or send me a "sympathy" invite, but I do know it's important for me to get out. I am not trying to date (I'm nowhere near ready for that) but would like to be included in dinner parties, etc. Any advice on how to handle this situation?

— *Lonely in Virginia*

DEAR LONELY: Developing and maintaining friendships is hard work. You need to initiate some social action — and put it out there for your friends.

By "putting it out there," I mean you need to inform (or remind) your friends that you'd like to get out more and that you're starving for adult socializing. If you aren't comfortable entertaining in your home, you could invite friends to a barbecue, ballgame or outdoor concert. Be honest with your friends and tell them you'd like to get out more but don't really know how to do it. Ask for their ideas and follow through.

Accept an invitation for what it is, even if you suspect it's a "sympathy" invite. Also accept that the "third wheel" dynamic goes with the territory — but it does change with time. During the school year, if you are able to coach a kids team (or assist another coach), this is a good way to meet other parents — especially guys.

You need male friends, but women and wives often control the family's social directory. Reach out, be honest and realize that much of the effort will be yours — but it is worth it. You might also benefit from meeting other single parents (when I was a single mom, many of my friends were also single parents). Parents Without Partners might be useful: parentswithoutpartners.org.

Neighborhood lighting causes awkwardness

DEAR AMY: We have new neighbors next door. Their home is the typical oversized structure for the size of the lot and has enough lighting in the front to light up a ballpark.

The lights continue to be on from dusk to dawn every day. They are wonderful and friendly people. How can I tell them that their lighting is literally keeping me up at night? It illuminates the entire front portion of my house, including the upstairs bedrooms.

— *Illuminated Neighbor*

DEAR ILLUMINATED: I frequently receive queries about how to facilitate conversation between neighbors.

Ask yourself how you would feel if something you did caused your neighbors distress and sleepless nights. Wouldn't you want to know about it in order to make some changes? All you have to do is tell the truth. Start by saying, "I'm embarrassed because I should have mentioned this sooner. Can you help me out here?" And then explain the problem.

Married man should include wife in relationship query

DEAR AMY: I haven't seen my lover from college for more than 40 years. We had a fun and intimate relationship for several months until she moved away to grad school. Shortly after the move, she called one day and to say that course work was too much to handle with a long-distance relationship and that she would likely never see me again. That was the last communication.

I have been thinking of her and wonder if I should contact her to catch up on life in general and chat about where we have taken our lives. Rekindling our romance is the furthest thing from my mind. Through the Internet, I know that she is now happily married with a family, mirroring my own situation.

In spite of my desire to see her again, my gut feeling is to just be content with fond memories of our time together and let it go at that. Should I see her again?

— *Just Wondering*

DEAR WONDERING: When faced with such a highly charged personal dilemma, I think it's best for a happily married man to ask his wife for her opinion.

Jack and Jill take hostages at dinner

DEAR AMY: My husband and I are in our mid-50s. We have a group of wonderful friends. We get together frequently as a group.

One of these couples worries me. I'll call them "Jack and Jill." Jack can be a great guy and very good company, but lately we have been forced to witness him making very crude, rude and sexually degrading comments mostly directed toward his wife. She will ask him to stop, and he usually does stop after a while. This seems to be happening more frequently and his comments are more crude.

We are so appalled that we don't know what to say, especially because other people are present. Honestly, we are hoping that Jack will read about himself in your column and that this will be a wake-up call for him. Do you have any other suggestions?

— *Worried Friends*

DEAR WORRIED: Your friend's behavior is surprising, disturbing and baffling. He is holding you (and everyone else present) hostage to his choices. And yet you don't report that anyone other than his wife is asking him to stop.

When someone is being publicly offensive, you can say, "Hey — whoa. I'd appreciate it if you would stop speaking that way. Thank you." After this, the person in your group who is closest to this man should speak to him privately to say, "What in the Sam Hill is going on with you?"

The person closest to his wife should also speak with her to make sure she is OK. This man might have a medical or emotional issue causing him to act out. He should be encouraged to get a thorough checkup as soon as possible.

Friend's gift of book tests tolerance

DEAR AMY: I have a friend whom I have not seen in decades. We were once very close, including being bridesmaids for each other, but we live far apart and our contact now consists of exchanging annual holiday greetings.

Our lives are very different. I married a "nice Jewish boy," and we lead a secular life that is rich with family dinners, lively conversations about personal and public ethics, and activism and service, particularly for social justice and economic equity.

She married an evangelical Christian, and they work as missionaries. Two or three times over the years, she has expressed concern about my life choices (including marrying a non-Christian) and how they will affect my chances of salvation. I've always let it go. But this year, she sent me a book, "an introduction" to accepting an evangelical lifestyle, with a note advising me to read the book and act by it.

You can imagine our family dinner conversations now, and my husband's and kids' reactions. We've considered sending it back with a note that says you must have mistakenly sent this to me; calling her and telling her I am offended; sending her the book "The God Delusion."

I could let it go, but my teenage son believes this is no different from a racist or sexist remark — something we would never overlook. What do you think I should do?

— *Wondering*

DEAR WONDERING: I think you should choose kindness and tolerance. The kindest, most accepting and "socially just" reaction would be to realize that your friend is a missionary. Missionaries spread the word. This is a core value for her.

I assume that your core values involve diversity of thought, action and freedom of religion (or from religion) — and so can you tolerate this religious expression from her? This is not akin to making a racist or sexist comment — though the implication, of course, is that you are on the "wrong" path and must be set right. That's no fun, to be sure.

This presents an opportunity for you to teach your children about accepting the views and behavior of people who are very different from you. The next topic for your household's dinner conversation might be titled: "It is very easy to take offense. Can we do otherwise?"

Young driver worries about baby transport

DEAR AMY: I'm a sophomore in high school. I have a sophomore friend who has an 11-month-old baby. For the past month, she has been asking me for rides. This involves taking her from the school to the day care center, waiting about 10 minutes there to pick up the baby and then taking her to her house. By that time, it's almost 3:45. I don't always have time to do this every day, and these past few weeks she's just kind of assuming that she has a ride. She doesn't even ask me anymore.

On top of all that, there's a safety issue. She doesn't buckle him in when they ride in my car, and sometimes faces him toward the front! And I obviously don't own a car-seat holder. I don't want to get in trouble for this if anything happened. I don't know how to approach this situation. Please help!

— Unsure

DEAR UNSURE: You should never, under any circumstances, transport a baby in your car untethered. Even if the baby is in a bucket-style portable carrier with a handle, the baby should be properly and securely strapped into the car — and always in the back seat.

If you are too young and timid to insist on this non-negotiable when you are the driver, then you shouldn't be driving this little family around. Take the safety issue as your primary reason to talk about this with your friend. I think it's absolutely great that you have been so helpful, and hope you can continue — on a schedule that works for you.

She must make sure you have the appropriate baby carrier properly installed in your car. These are readily available secondhand, and the people at your local fire department will be happy to check it and help you install it securely.

And where, oh where, are your parents (yours and hers)? Your friend needs very basic parenting instruction, and you need help to assert yourself over what is a very important safety issue.

Fellow gym goer makes workouts extra-strenuous

DEAR AMY: In our athletic club, there is one lady who has a rather loud, irritating voice and unfortunately spends an hour or more on one elliptical machine. She never shuts up. Unfortunately her voice carries almost all over the gym, so if one wants to read and doesn't have a $300 pair of earphones which totally block out her noise, it is nearly impossible to concentrate.

She is a nice lady, and I think no one wants to hurt her feelings, but it is very annoying and disturbing. I have tried earplugs and loud music via iPod, but these, too, are ineffective. The club supposedly does not allow cellphones to be used on the machines, but believe me, she talks louder than anyone on any cellphone. Any suggestions?

— *Hoping for Silence*

DEAR HOPING: My great suggestion is for you to find your own voice and use your words to simply say, "I'm sorry, but would you mind lowering your voice? It is hard for me to concentrate when I can overhear your conversation."

After that, if your request falls upon deaf ears, it is your club's responsibility to make sure that all members adhere to basic guidelines while they are using the club's facilities.

No easy way to end a friendship

DEAR AMY: What is the kindest way to let a person know that you are no longer interested in a friendship? A former friend (at least that's how I feel) continues to send emails and leave phone messages, which I haven't returned in the hopes that she gets the hint.

However, it appears that it hasn't occurred to her that I no longer want to pursue a friendship with her.

Having known her for a number of years, I do feel as if I may owe her an explanation, but I fear that there is no nice way to say to someone, "I don't want to be your friend anymore" or is there?

— *Former Friend*

DEAR FORMER: Breaking up is hard to do, and breaking up with a friend is in some ways harder than severing a romantic attachment because of the length and breadth of the relationship. And yet, breaking up is the right thing to do.

Imagine how you would feel if you were laboring along, extending yourself through friendship and oblivious to the fact that someone was dodging and wanted to dump you? You don't mention reasons why you want to leave this friendship, and so I suggest a version of "It's not you; it's me."

You should call her to say, "I feel terrible because I haven't been completely honest with you. I am sorry, but I just feel our friendship has run its course, and I no longer have anything to offer." If she is a lovely person who deserves better, tell her so. If she has done specific things that have affected you and that you can't get past, then tell her that too. And if she has something to say, listen. The painful penance of delivering the breakup is to face the person's reaction.

Marrying couple worries about gift registry

DEAR AMY: I recently got married. In addition to registering for traditional items, my husband and I decided to include two charities. We never thought anything of this, other than the potential good it could do. However, I was just reading through an online wedding forum, and many people thought it was rude to ask guests to donate to charity. They said a wedding was not a time to discuss "depressing" things.

These people equated charity registries to just asking for cash. They assumed that brides who went this route were arrogant. My opinion is that even a registry asking for blenders and steak knives is asking for "money," so why not do the world a little good? Was I in the wrong? Is it tacky?

— *New Bride*

DEAR BRIDE: Registries are all about directing guests' giving toward what the marrying couple wants to receive. Many guests find registries very helpful, though guests can always choose to ignore a registry.

My reaction to your choice to include nonprofits is not that this is "depressing" (far from it), but perhaps a little confusing. It's as if you are including a grab bag of opposing ideas for guests. However, this was your wedding. Many couples use their nuptials to inspire guests to raise money for charity, and I don't think it's tacky at all — it's lovely. Now, stay off the wedding message boards. Nothing good can come of it.

Gay high school student wants to act on crush

DEAR AMY: I am a 17-year-old girl in high school. I am also gay. I have a good friend I have known since elementary school. I have a crush on her, and I don't quite know how to tell her how I feel. She gives mixed signals. She doesn't know that I'm gay. If I say the wrong thing, it could seriously affect our friendship.

— *Puzzled Friend*

DEAR PUZZLED: If your friend doesn't know you are gay, the most obvious first step is to tell her. She may be sending out mixed signals, but you may also be misinterpreting her behavior. Telling her you have a crush on her without her knowing you are gay could be extremely confusing.

Teen worries about friend's reaction to cancer

DEAR AMY: I am a freshman in high school. Last summer my best friend was diagnosed with skin cancer. It wasn't very serious, but it took a definite toll on her.

I have been supportive and encouraging, and I've stood by her when times are tough. Recently she found out the scar she has from it won't ever go away. She seems to be becoming more and more sad. She has started looking at all the negatives in life, and sometimes it brings me down too. What I'm wondering is: How can I cheer her up?

I want her to be happy again. What do you say to someone with cancer, and how can I help change her outlook on life?

— *Best Friend*

DEAR FRIEND: Your best role is to prop up and encourage your friend when she seems down, and to be supportive and kind to her. You're doing a great job with that, and your friend is lucky to have you in her life. But some things are beyond your abilities, and that is when the adults in her life should step in and become more involved.

Her sadness and negativity may not be directly related to her brush with serious illness. She sounds depressed, and she should see a doctor for an evaluation. Reach out to a trusted adult to share your concerns; disclose exactly what you are observing, and say you are worried about her and that you believe she needs help.

As designated driver, get keys early

DEAR AMY: I know that "friends don't let friends drive drunk," but the last few times I've been in a situation in which I've offered to drive or call a cab for friends who'd been drinking, they've insisted they were "OK to drive." One friend was so obviously impaired that I refused to get into her car and ended up walking.

She was angry with me, and we didn't speak for some time after the incident. Recently, a different acquaintance had been giggling about how "tipsy" she was but refused my offer to drive her home, and when I texted the next day to see if she'd made it home safely, she was irritated and said she never would have driven if she didn't think she was OK.

Amy, these are professional women in their 40s. I don't think I'm coming across as judgmental when I offer; I'm actually pretty non-confrontational. In fact, I think I should be more assertive and just take their keys, but I don't know how. Can you suggest any sort of tried and true script I could follow that would be effective in convincing people that even if they feel "OK" it's not worth taking the chance?

— *Sober Friend*

DEAR SOBER: First off, you are not responsible for your friends' atrocious and dangerous behavior. You attempted to intervene and drive a drunken friend home; when she declined, you were very wise to walk.

I shared your query with Dorene Ocamb, spokeswoman for Mothers Against Drunk Driving (madd.org), and we agree that a more assertive way to approach this would be to agree before the drinking starts that you will be the designated driver. The friend would relinquish her keys at the beginning of the evening, thus sparing you the impossible task of trying to lasso an inebriated friend.

Drunk or impaired people often report that they are "fine," but they are impaired and are in no condition to judge their own sobriety. Ocamb adds, "The other alternative — and we only suggest this with hesitation — is that you have the option of calling the police. You have to figure out what's right for you and for your relationship."

Once you disclose this to her, you should wait for a couple of weeks to see how she reacts to this news. She may be interested in having a different kind of relationship with you, but you should be prepared that she may not want this.

Mystery baby has neighbor concerned

DEAR AMY: I am in a quandary about whether I should mind my own business about a situation in our neighborhood. A neighbor had a baby a year ago, announced with a banner on their front porch. We did not know she was pregnant. They keep to themselves. That baby has never been seen by the neighbors, not even their next-door neighbor.

They never bring her outside, and no one has seen the child (or the parents) in their yard. Other neighbors have had babies in the last three years, and they all play outside with one another. We have seen them take the baby out in the car maybe three or four times.

Attempts by various neighbors to be friendly are quietly rebuffed at the door. I'm wondering whether to make a call to Children's Protective Services to request a welfare check on the child. Staying indoors 24/7 can't be healthy for a baby.

— *Worried Neighbor*

DEAR WORRIED: This child could have health (or other) problems causing the parents to keep the baby inside; you simply don't know. You also don't know what this family's lifestyle or work schedule is.

Over the years, many people have contacted me to say they grew up in terrible circumstances in a neighborhood where "not one person intervened." While I do not suggest being a busybody or necessarily judging choices parents make, our child welfare system is set up to be the advocate for children who cannot advocate for themselves.

If you are truly worried about this baby's health, safety and welfare, and if you have tried other ways and cannot determine whether the child is OK, then you should make the call.

Generous giver creates imbalance

DEAR AMY: I am a grad student with somewhat limited funds. I save up for really nice presents for my friends for Christmas, and I try to make the gifts personal. I've always done this because I want that person to feel special. Although my friends make decent incomes, it's clear that they don't spend very much on presents and don't make them personal.

I know it is the thought that counts, but it seems to me that they didn't put much thought into it at all! I wish I didn't feel hurt by this, but I do. What should I do?

—*Disappointed*

DEAR DISAPPOINTED: You need to explore why you are giving gifts. Are your gifts a reflection of your tastes and values and an expression of your natural generosity, or do you use gifts to inspire other people to give equally to you?

You should not put more money or time into your gift-giving than you have to spare — happily, willingly and without expectation. When you free yourself from an expectation of reciprocity, you may end up adjusting your giving so it's less stressful for you. You will definitely receive more pure joy from the act of giving.

Old school friend tries too hard

DEAR AMY: I lost touch with a very good friend from high school and have been trying to locate her for seven years. I've searched the Internet, asked mutual friends and even contacted her parents via mail but never received a response.

I also left a phone message at her parents' home. I know the phone number was good because their names and voices were on the outgoing message. It seems that there is a lot more going on and that they are deliberately trying to keep their daughter "hidden." It just seems odd. They knew me from elementary school until we graduated.

I would think that if their daughter didn't want to get in touch they could at least acknowledge my letter and let me know that she's not interested in getting back in touch. We didn't leave on bad terms; we just grew apart.

I really miss her, but I can't get a response (much less find her), and the not knowing what happened to her is driving me crazy. Should I give up? Has too much time passed? Should I just accept that she doesn't want to get in contact? Or should I keep reaching out in hopes she will eventually contact me back?

— *Missing My Old Friend*

DEAR MISSING: I suggest you stop before somebody gets a constable involved. You have tried every reasonable means possible to contact this person from your past. Aside from hopping onto Facebook to see if she has an account (you don't mention doing this), you should take all of this nonresponse from family and mutual friends to mean that she does not want to be in touch. You should accept and respect this lack of contact for what it is — a mystery — and move on.

Does vow renewal dictate gift renewal?

DEAR AMY: We have good friends who are renewing their vows next month. I'm not a fan of these ceremonies, but we wouldn't miss something that is important to them. We received a somewhat formal invitation, including a response card. The ceremony and barbecue reception will be at their house.

Are we supposed to take a gift — just like the first time they recited their vows?

— *Former Matron of Honor*

DEAR FORMER: I vote no on a gift. However, I do think you should dig up a photo from this couple's original wedding, if possible, and write a fun and sweet caption on it. You could note that styles may change and hairlines may recede, but a long and happy marriage never goes out of style.

Illness creates inconstant relationships

DEAR AMY: A friend of mine died recently after a long battle with cancer. She had been a very social person until the last year of her life when she was too sick to get out much. During her last year, many of her lifelong friends dropped her.

I continued to call her several times a week, took her to the movies and shopping, and when she couldn't go out, I stopped by her home and brought her books or pastries that she liked. She told me how lonely she was and asked that I call specific friends and ask them to visit her. Two friends increased their visits. All of the others said they wouldn't go to see her because it was too hard on them.

This makes me angry; after all, they are alive and well and knew that our friend wouldn't be with us much longer. Some of these "friends" had known her since childhood. It might hurt me to see her dying, but think how much it must have hurt her to know that her friends wouldn't come to see her in her last months!

— *Morgan*

DEAR MORGAN: Modern life has removed most of us so thoroughly from the real stuff of life that many people simply don't believe they can cope with being exposed to physical suffering and its attendant confusion and sadness.

They can cope with it, but they don't know it, and their anxiety gives them "cover" to stay away. You sound like a good and constant friend. You might have helped some of your more reluctant friends to step up by bringing them along with you to show them how to have a good visit with someone who is ill.

Some people also cope better when given a specific job. Your friends who found this "too hard" might have been more comfortable providing a weekly meal or doing errands for your ill friend.

Young mom's life creates conference calls

DEAR AMY: I have a lifelong friend who is the mother of an energetic 3½ year old boy. We used to speak several times a day by phone about basically — nothing. It was just chatter.

Now whenever any of her friends call her, we have a multiway conversation with her, her husband and/or the little guy. It is impossible to have a conversation of any kind at any time! What is a tactful way to approach this without hurting the friendship? We all have tried calling while her son is napping, but it's as if he has radar! When her husband is home, he chimes in. We now speak maybe 2–3 times a week, and I miss our talks.

— Going Crazy

DEAR CRAZY: You say you used to enjoy your multiple opportunities for meaningless chatter. But now when you call your friend and actually get meaningless chatter, you say you don't like it.

Cut this mom some slack. She simply can't be available to you the way she once was. This will change in time. Urge your friend to call you when she can, but don't push her into having the kind of contact with you she can no longer have. A "girls' night out" might be the best way to get your meaningless chatter back.

Life Online

Screwing Up Across Platforms

When friendship fades, exit quietly

DEAR AMY: I've been best friends with "Molly" since we were children. We're now in our early 20s. We've been very close and have always shared our ups and downs.

She has suffered from an eating disorder for a few years now. She's received help, but her life seems to be a roller coaster.

I've tried being there for her, but she has a tendency to shut down and block me out. She has ditched me at the last minute on many occasions without any notice. Then she ignores me for a few weeks or a few months. This hurts me. I don't have many friends, and I worry about her.

When she finally communicates with me, she says she's "just been having a rough time lately," but she will post pictures on Facebook of her activities during these times, and I see that she seems to be busy with other friends.

This friendship is held up only by me, and I think I've had enough. She hasn't talked to me for more than a month now. I deleted her off Facebook because I got annoyed seeing her interacting with all of her other friends, except for me. Should I communicate my feelings — or leave her wondering? That's how she always treats me, so maybe I should show her what it feels like.

— *Angry*

DEAR ANGRY: If your friend suffers from anxiety or depression, this would compel her to pull away periodically, and it would be a mistake for you to take it personally. However, given the fact that this relationship is depleting you, you should — finally — act only on your own behalf and not attempt to manipulate Molly.

If you try to make her wonder about you, I guarantee that she will not wonder about you. If you try to retaliate in some way, this negative energy will only bounce back and hit you in the gut, because she may lack the capacity to notice.

If it would make you feel better to express your disappointment in her, then do it. If it would make you feel better to simply fade away, then definitely do that.

Secret online relationship raises red flags

DEAR AMY: I'm a girl in high school and I have a bit of a problem. Last year I was bored and went on a website and ended up meeting this guy (who is my age). We've been texting, calling and Skyping ever since. I really like this guy, but I've never actually met him in person, and he lives in a different state.

First of all, is it worth having feelings for someone you might not meet for years and who you don't get to actually hang out with? I've come to look forward to talking to him every day and don't know what I'd do if it stopped. I hope he or my parents don't see this.

— *Wondering*

DEAR WONDERING: You almost had me — until your last sentence. There's nothing wrong with having a long-distance relationship, and it's increasingly common for people who have never met in person to engage through phone, Facebook, text and Skype. This particular relationship raises all sorts of red flags (for instance, you likely aren't able to verify a single thing about each other). It is also impeding your motivation to do the hard work to meet and interact with people in person. But the most important thing about it is the secrecy. It is wrong to have a secret relationship. It just is.

Older man with young libido worries about wife

DEAR AMY: I am a man in my upper 70s. I still have a relatively strong libido. My wife, same age, is quite ill and has no ability or interest in any sexual behavior.

As a result, I find some satisfaction in perusing erotic Internet sites and also a free site in which one can chat with people about sexual matters. From a moral standpoint I am sure this is not good conduct, but practically I feel it is of some help to me and involves no risk of disease since I do not pursue any real-world sexual conduct. Do you have an opinion? Should I seek help in discarding this behavior?

— *Codger*

DEAR CODGER: You don't say what your wife thinks of this, but to me your conduct doesn't seem any more in need of correction than a person who chooses to read Playboy, D.H. Lawrence or the latest Harlequin bodice-ripper. If these Internet sites feature adults engaging in consensual and legal activity, then peruse away. The "chatting" gives me pause, however. This will complicate matters and lead to an emotional involvement.

Facebook creates unfriendly dilemma

DEAR AMY: I have been friends with a woman for most of my life. We lived across the street from each other growing up, and through the years we have kept in touch with annual Christmas cards. We haven't seen each other or spoken personally in many years. Last year, her 15-year-old daughter "Julia" "friended" me on Facebook, and I accepted.

She seemed interested in knowing some of her mother's friends, and I thought she contacted me as another way for her mother to keep in touch with me. Her mother does not have a Facebook account. During the year, Julia posted several messages that seemed to indicate she was a little depressed or angry. She's also in a heavy romance with a boy at school. I asked if there was anything wrong, and she replied that sometimes life was frustrating but it wasn't anything she couldn't handle.

On Christmas Eve, she posted a very vulgar and sexually explicit passage. It ended up on my Facebook wall and news feed for all of my contacts to see. After she admitted writing the passage, I told her it was disgusting and she really shouldn't post things like that because they can live forever even if deleted. The girl promptly "unfriended" me, blocked me and changed her screen name.

Should I call her mother and tell her what happened? The mother may dump me too, and I would feel bad. On the other hand, she may want to know what her daughter has been up to.

— *Concerned Old Friend*

DEAR CONCERNED: "Julia" behaved like an adolescent girl, and you reacted like a grown-up. Good for you. Julia's behavior since your admonition is also age-appropriate. She is running for cover. You can only hope she is embarrassed and has learned from this experience. If you have some evidence that this young person is engaged in behavior that is actually dangerous (and not just to her reputation), then you should definitely and emphatically reach out to this parent.

Otherwise, you can use this as a reason to reach out in friendship to the mother, not to tattle on the daughter, but to check in. You can say to this mom, "Julia and I were Facebook friends for a while, but then she dropped off the screen, so now I have to contact you the old-fashioned way. How are you both doing?"

On Facebook, breaking up is hard

DEAR AMY: Over seven months have passed since my boyfriend of almost a year and I broke up. Since that time he has dated two other women. He has been with his current girlfriend for several months. I'm also seeing someone. I understand a certain amount of trash talking occurs after a breakup, but I feel he's been inappropriate, and I'm not sure how to handle the situation.

I've left him alone and have refrained from airing what I disliked about our relationship to the general public. He, on the other hand, has talked to my boyfriend about why he shouldn't date me and recently publicly bashed me on his Facebook page. This includes calling me a "constant embarrassment," mentioning a much-regretted trip to the hospital due to an alcohol overdose (which is highly personal and happened a long time ago). He is publicly exaggerating events from my past.

I sent him a cordial message expressing how this post has hurt my feelings and is inappropriate, and he hasn't responded or taken action to delete this very public post. What should I do?

— *Facebooked*

DEAR FACEBOOKED: I shared your query with Nicky Colaco, a representative of Facebook, who noted that Facebook's terms of service specify that users should not post offensive or malicious content.

"We encourage people to let us know when they see something they think might violate our standards," Colaco wrote. "Our team of investigators reviews and takes action on reported content according to our policies."

Your boyfriend's postings qualify as malicious, at least in my view, because the intent is to personally disparage you. You can report this by clicking the "Report" button on the Facebook page. You can also distance yourself by blocking him on Facebook. Otherwise you should not publicly comment on or have any contact with your ex. His actions constitute an aggressive and obvious statement about the kind of person he is.

Keeping tabs on Facebook photos

DEAR AMY: I would like some advice about how to let friends and family know that I would not like any pictures of my family posted on Facebook or any other social networking site. What the heck is the best way to do this without sounding like a freak?

— *Concerned*

DEAR CONCERNED: I remember back at the dawn of Facebook (say, two or three years ago) when I advocated in this space for the concept of "permission" regarding the posting of photos. Oh, how young and naive I was. Now I'm on Facebook myself, and I know better.

By all means, ask people in your circle not to post photos of your family on social networking sites. Your friends won't think you're a freak; they'll just think you're being unrealistic. The people in your personal circle of actual "friends" may go to great lengths to respect your wishes — but then there are your kids' friends; their teammates; their teammates' moms and their teammate's mom's sister-in-law, Brenda, who took some awesome pictures of the kids during their last game and has posted and "tagged" all the children in the photos.

Join these sites yourself. This is the best way to patrol what photos are floating around. Then you can attempt to control them, by removing "tags" or asking people to pull photos down.

Unfriend this Facebook 'friend'

DEAR AMY: I have a dear friend I've known for 30 years. She lives in another town. I've also known her father and stepmother for many years. Recently my friend's father friended me on Facebook. I was happy at first, but he writes diatribes to almost anything I post and has used (somewhat "coded") obscene language. It's really weird.

I asked him not to use the language, and he seems to have backed off a bit, but he spends way too much time on Facebook and way too much time "challenging" me on political and religious stuff. How can I stop it?

— *Facebooked*

DEAR FACEBOOKED: You could unfriend or block him (if he routinely spams people with obscene or aggressive responses, he has probably already been blocked by others), but if you feel this would cause additional unpleasantness, you could limit his access to your posts.

There is a little lock-shaped icon to the lower right of the "status update" on Facebook. You can use this feature to control who sees your posts. This enables you to basically shimmy around the question of blocking this person. You two would still be Facebook friends, but if he doesn't see your posts, he won't have much to push against.

Cringe-worthy whines on Facebook

DEAR AMY: My daughter-in-law "Wendy" uses Facebook to complain. Her entries focus on how much she hates her job, her boss, how much she feels cheated by being a working mother, and even a post or two about the shortcomings of her new husband (my son), who apparently failed to buy her a lavish enough Mother's Day present.

These posts create a kind of online persona that makes her seem almost vicious, and she really isn't that way. At least I never thought so before. But the really embarrassing part is that she is Facebook "friends" with everyone in my family, and believe me, her posts are a topic of not-too-flattering gossip, along with some outright concern.

My son is not on Facebook. I have mentioned to him a few times when her posts have become offensive, and he is trying to deal with it offline. Should I offer to have a talk with my daughter-in-law? Or just hope my son figures this out?

— *Concerned Mother-in-law*

DEAR CONCERNED: When your daughter-in-law posts her complaints, selfishness or negativity on the public bulletin board that is Facebook, she runs the risk of ruining her personal and professional reputation. And that's her business.

When her whining veers into family territory, that's your business. You can assume that because her public online persona is unpleasant, your son is aware of her unpleasantness in the private, personal arena.

A gentle and respectful "heads-up" (to her) is in order — and then you should back off, adjust your settings (both metaphorically and on Facebook) and stop reading her posts. You can say to her, "I'm worried about some of your postings, especially when you write negative things about family members. It can create some hurt feelings, and I'm sure that's not your intent."

Internet affair exposes marriage flaws

DEAR AMY: My husband had an Internet affair with his high school sweetheart from 40 years ago. He says that it is over, that he loves me but is not in love with me. He moved out to see if he can "rekindle" his love for me. He still wants to see me and "date."

He isn't giving me any money for expenses. He owes me money but denies it. Despite all this, I love him and want to be with him. I've been trying to keep things light, but my heart is breaking. What should I do?

— *Hates High School*

DEAR HIGH SCHOOL: Moving out is a curious way to rekindle the relationship. Your husband has left your marital home. He loves you as a person but is not "in love" with you (mind you, he could say the same thing about Betty White).

You and your husband are separated. I suggest you consider making it official. You should see a lawyer to review your (and his) rights and responsibilities. You should not have to keep things light to lure him back. Date him if you must, but protect yourself.

Teen faces Facebook consequences

DEAR AMY: I am a 15-year-old girl. I have known my friend "James" for 10 years. We are close. We attend the same school and church. Our religion is against gay marriage.

A few days ago, I was on Facebook, but it was logged into my friend "Tiffany's" account. I didn't realize I was logged into her account until I read a message that James sent her. James told Tiffany that he was gay. He said he didn't know how to come out and tell other people. He was also slamming our religion.

He has been called gay since sixth grade but always denied it. He seemed hurt by the accusation. I told my sister what I found out, and then she told my father. My dad told James' dad, and the whole thing got back to James. James now hates me and won't talk to me.

He says that I shouldn't have been looking through Tiffany's messages, and that I should have kept the news about him to myself. I am really hurt. I told him the whole story, but he doesn't believe me. Was I wrong for telling my sister? I still love James, but I don't agree with his lifestyle. What can I do to fix our friendship?

— *Sad Teen*

DEAR TEEN: "James" is right. Though it is possible to be on Facebook under someone else's account without necessarily realizing it, you read your friend's private message and then after you knew this message was private, you disclosed it to someone else. When you are close friends with someone, you should take your personal questions and concerns directly to the friend — and not to others.

This is a very sensitive issue that concerns an important disclosure. James has serious questions about how to communicate with his family. He now doesn't have the option to make his own choice about how to talk about his private life because you and your family have made this choice for him.

You are young, and you've made a mistake. The most you can do now is also the best thing to do — always. Tell the truth. Acknowledge your mistake. Ask for forgiveness and hope it will be granted to you.

Snooping ex violated friendship

DEAR AMY: I am 24. Four months ago I broke up with my boyfriend of almost three years. It was really hard for me to break up, but I had to do it.

To make a long story short, I kissed a new guy less than two weeks after the breakup. We started dating, and we're still together. I knew this all happened unusually soon, so out of sensitivity for my ex's feelings I tried to keep the information private. I had told only a few close friends in private Facebook messages.

Unfortunately I did not realize that my Facebook password was still saved on my ex's computer, so you can guess what happened! I am very angry that my ex would read my private messages. He didn't just "peek" once; he continued to read them for more than a month!

Now he uses every private word I typed against me. He says that because of what I have done, he doesn't think we can ever be friends. I feel bad that the information my ex found has hurt him so badly, yet I'm pretty angry that he snooped. Have I done wrong here? Can we be friends?

— *Ex*

DEAR EX: I find that the person who initiates the breakup often moves on quite quickly, and the injured party frequently doesn't like it. That doesn't make it "wrong." That makes it ... life.

Snooping is a hurtful violation. So no, you probably can't be friends. At least not now. But then, it doesn't seem that you have any incentive to be friends with your ex.

Staying friendly with ex's family

DEAR AMY: Over the summer, I reached out to an ex of mine whom I've never really gotten over. His response was not favorable. I've come to terms with the fact that there is no chance of a romantic reconciliation between us. But over the past decade, I've remained in contact with his family, especially his mother and sister, who are lovely people.

We email a few times a year and send Christmas and sometimes birthday cards. After this summer's exchange, I "unfriended" my ex's mother and sister from Facebook. At the time, it was too painful for me to see photos of him and hear updates about him.

Now six months have passed, and I received both a birthday greeting and a Christmas card from his sister. I feel bad for cutting off contact with no explanation. What should I do, Amy? Should I explain to them what happened? Re-friend them without explanation? Remain silent on Facebook but continue sending birthday and holiday greetings?

— *Reconsidering*

DEAR RECONSIDERING: You don't need to explain your feelings about your ex — this falls into the category of "private business" between you two — and you can assume that his family members probably understand some of your sensitivities without your spelling them out.

If being Facebook friends triggers tough emotions for you, then it is best to leave these people off your "friends" list. However, real-world friendships should transcend this awkwardness. I suggest you continue to be in occasional contact with these people because you are fond of them — and they are obviously fond of you.

Internet match upset about discretion

DEAR AMY: I recently posted my profile on a few dating sites. I'm 18 years old and would love to meet a nice guy. I connected with a "match." He expressed interest in emailing, but I didn't want to use my personal address so I created a new address with a fake last name for my own personal safety.

We have chatted almost every night since, and today I felt that it was time to tell him my real name, and I wrote him an explanatory email, giving my reasons and apologizing profusely. He is upset now, and said he doesn't feel like he can trust me because he was honest with me from the beginning. I told him that any contact would have to be initiated by him, but I feel like I've lost my best friend.

Was I wrong to create this email with a fake name — or is he over-reacting?

— *Unsure*

DEAR UNSURE: You didn't need to assume a secret identity — you only needed to leave off your last name on any communication until you wanted to disclose it. That having been said, this guy is overreacting.

Please, always proceed very cautiously when it comes to forming relationships online. Don't get too wrapped up in an online relationship before you meet the person, and always meet for coffee (no alcohol) in a public place.

Secret email account stirs suspicion

DEAR AMY: Five years ago, I saw my wife's social website profile, which implied she was single. She refused to talk about it, so I put a keystroke logger on our computer and caught her in a one-night stand with a friend from high school. She swore she would never do it again, offered me her passwords and closed her Facebook account.

Two years later, I became suspicious again. Again she avoided talking, so I put a tape recorder in her car and discovered she had been going to a motel with another married man. A few weeks ago, I was dropping a movie off at the library when I noticed my wife was on a public computer. She was obviously flustered when I said hello.

Yesterday, I had a friend go to the library to see what she was doing. She was emailing, but from a secret email account. I knew her passwords for her four other email accounts. Is her using a secret email account justified?

I was slowly beginning to trust her again, but seeing her sneaking to the library every day to use a public computer seems like a huge setback. Is it better to find out if she is having an affair first or talk (and fight) now, when I can only confirm this secret computer usage? We have two children, and I'm afraid of acting prematurely. But if it's another affair, I definitely want out now.

— *Hurt Husband*

DEAR HURT: Your wife is a chronic liar, and you have responded with surveillance. I don't necessarily blame you — she's asking for it — but it's not yielding the result you desire. So stop. You can't prove your wife's innocence. At this point, given her history, that's her job.

Your task now is to figure out what you should do next. If you think you must stay together for the sake of the kids, re-read your letter and ponder the lessons they are learning from their folks. It's time for you to see a counselor and a lawyer.

You might suggest to your wife that the next time she's at the library, she should bring home a book for you: "Divorce for Dummies," by John Ventura and Mary Reed (2009, For Dummies). This might compel her to talk.

Facebook flirting has wife hurting

DEAR AMY: My husband and I have been married for 25 years. We have a happy marriage, except for one issue. For the past three years, since joining Facebook, my husband has been contacting former girlfriends. He does background searches on them: whom they married, what their spouses look like, where they work and property information to see where they live and how much their homes are worth. He then starts to communicate with them, delving into personal and emotional aspects of their lives.

I accidentally discovered this when his cellphone alarm went off and I saw a text message from a woman I had never heard of. There were hundreds of messages between the two of them. They had switched from Facebook to texting to avoid detection from her husband. There was nothing overtly sexual (only flirty), and he asked her to send a picture from when she was a cheerleader in high school.

I insisted he stop communicating with her, which he did. A few months later I discovered that he had created another account and a dossier of pictures of her from high school and from Facebook, along with his background research. In the past year, he has done this at least six times with other women. One is a complete stranger (not someone from his past).

When I tell him this makes me very uncomfortable, he clams up and then accuses me of being jealous and controlling. He tells me there is nothing sexual going on, and says he has never been unfaithful (I agree). Should this not bother me? He says I have no right to tell him whom he can communicate with.

— *Anxious Spouse*

DEAR ANXIOUS: Your husband is right — you have no right to tell him whom he can communicate with. But embedded within the emotional contract of marriage is the implicit agreement that spouses will make every effort not to cause their partner pain or anxiety.

His "investigations" and dossiers are creepy. Delving into emotional and intimate conversations with these women definitely crosses the line. His secrecy tells you that he knows this is wrong. I gather he does not do this with male friends from high school. Why not?

Vegan unwittingly creates meat-hating comedy

DEAR AMY: I have a friend who recently decided to become vegetarian/vegan. She now shares articles via email and Facebook calling people who eat meat "depraved," "confused" and "unethical." There was even an article accusing meat eaters of being "species-ist."

I couldn't care less about her diet, but how should I deal with the vicious language she's using toward people like me who do eat meat? Every time I try to talk to her about it, she thinks I'm somehow disagreeing with vegetarianism, which is not the case.

— *Offended Omnivore*

DEAR OFFENDED: It would be fairly easy to block or "hide" these messages. If you don't want to do this, I suggest you alter your own attitude and see these diatribes for what they are: vegetarian comedy. If you insist that these polemics are hilarious you might be able to enjoy them — with a nice steak and a glass of merlot.

Brother's Skype causes sibling gripe

DEAR AMY: My brother (we share a bedroom) stays up till 4 a.m. talking on Skype and using the computer when he is not supposed to. This happens every night.

In the morning I always wake up exhausted and wanting a nap. My grades are tanking; I don't have any energy during the day; and I get yelled at a lot because of this. The worst part is, when I tell my parents that he's up all night, they just say, "We've told him he can't do that" and insist that he is not up all night.

They disregard his misbehavior all the time and then take away my computer for slipping grades. How can I get my parents to believe me about my brother? I'd like my life back.

— *Sleepless in Seattle*

DEAR SLEEPLESS: First things first — your grades, your sleep, etc., are your responsibility.

I'm on your side here, but if your sleep is disrupted night after night, then you should try whatever remedies are available to deal with it. I'm talking about earplugs, night shades or sleeping on the couch.

Skype (the Internet calling service) keeps a tally of when calls were placed and their duration. Your parents should verify this usage by checking the program on your brother's computer. As the mother of teens (and former teens) I know that the 24-hour lure of constant contact is simply too much for some people to handle responsibly (I include myself in this category).

People should "unplug" at night. For people who can't manage this, laptops and smartphones should be brought down to the kitchen at bedtime and they should stay there until morning.

Facebook postings offend girl's aunt

DEAR AMY: I have a niece who is 18. She and I are "friends" on Facebook. The other day on my news feed, a video she posted of a pornographic nature (nudity and sexual activity involving a male stripper) popped up.

This is not the first time she has posted such things, but it is the worst. Another time she had a conversation with a male friend about "having his baby."

I am concerned for this girl but not sure how to approach her. We live far away from each other. Her mother, who I was very close to, died recently. I am not as close to her father. Do you have any suggestions? I do not want to be "unfriended."

— *Worried Aunt*

DEAR AUNT: For now, you should not comment on these posts. You might gain some insight, however, by reading through the comments made by others. Other Facebook "friends" and contemporaries may comment, "Wow — that's a little raw, don't you think?" or question her taste or judgment.

Facebook comments sometimes lead a person to self-correct. I do not think it's wise for you to comment publicly: "I find this highly offensive. Love you, Auntie" because, given your niece's immaturity, she will be done with you quickly, and you want to keep the door open.

If these posts worry (in addition to offend) you, you could send her a private message on Facebook to say, "Hi, I'm checking in. How are you doing lately?" Keep it benign and open-ended. You want to learn what she's thinking about, not just what she's posting, and develop enough intimacy with her that you can eventually ask her to reflect on how she's presenting herself online.

Subject of unfriending doesn't get it

DEAR AMY: I'm 60 and consider myself computer literate and socially mature, but I find myself stymied by a recent Facebook incident.

I'm a mentor to group of 20- and 30-somethings at my church. We socialize several times a month. We are all on Facebook. Recently one member "unfriended" three of us. She has explained this by saying she was just uncluttering her page and getting rid of contacts she had no contact with. However, the three of us see her, have exchanged gifts and have had her in our homes, all within the past year.

I've sent two emails and left one phone message to ask if I had inadvertently offended her, offering to meet for coffee to resolve this.

I also sent a new "friend" request. All of these have been ignored. When I've run into her with a group, she has hugged me but has made no other contact. I know it's just Facebook, but it feels very awkward. How do others handle unfriending?

— *Left Behind*

DEAR LEFT BEHIND: I posted a version of this question on my own Facebook page, and the response was large — and almost unanimous. One person wrote: "If I am 'unfriended,' I do nothing. If I talk to this person on a regular basis, then I assume that they find my updates and pictures boring. If I don't really talk to this person and don't really see them in real life, then it's no big deal. It's only Facebook."

You have an explanation from this person that is completely plausible. For some people, following the ongoing timelines of dozens (or hundreds) of people doesn't feel like "friendship" — but more like being an audience member.

Unfriending doesn't mean she doesn't like you but that she doesn't want to interact with you in this way. Your unwillingness to accept this provides a window onto the dynamic. Your response — to double up with more contact — is disrespectful. Step away from the keyboard, and accept this change gracefully.

Can online love lead to real thing?

DEAR AMY: I am an 18-year-old guy. I recently met a girl online through social networking. We started communicating a few weeks ago and have contacted each other every day since. We go to college, but in different states. Things are starting to get pretty serious, but other than video chatting we have never actually met.

We tell each other that we love each other, but I can't help but wonder how long this can possibly last. I really do love her, but with both of us being so busy I'm not sure when we will actually be able to meet. Is this really all that is "out there" in terms of hope for our future?

— *Concerned With the Future*

DEAR CONCERNED: It is definitely possible to feel you've fallen in love virtually, but sometimes this intense attraction and connection fades fairly quickly once you actually meet. If you can't meet in person soon, then you should back away from the intensity of this until you can meet.

There are so many intangibles to "real" love that it is hard to imagine that what you perceive as an 18-year-old virtually is even in the same ballpark as the real thing, because online relationships are like relationships between versions of people.

Sometimes people are better, and sometimes they're worse than in real life. But they're always different. I wonder why you are spending your hours communicating with someone so far away when surely there is the potential for you to interact (in person) with people who might become great friends (and maybe more) if you were available.

Adolescent boy Googles with guilt

DEAR AMY: My sweet 11-year-old son, who has started to hit puberty, confessed to me in a fit of tears that when I had left him at home with an older sister while I went to the store, he "went crazy." He told me he drank a can of soda (restricted at our house) and then he Googled pictures of naked girls on the Internet. He was distraught. He said he didn't know why he did it — it was like some other person was inside him and he couldn't control it. He'd been living with it for three days, worried I would find out, so he had to tell me.

Part of me is horrified and sad that my little boy saw these images (and horrified that he did it.) Then part of me thinks about what I'd read about boys in puberty — that the jolts of testosterone are like mainline drugs that leave a boy with very poor impulse control. I'm so proud of him for coming clean with me. But I wonder if I should be worried. We agreed on a punishment, and I was calm in expressing my disappointment. My goal is to keep him coming to me if he needs to confide to me in the future.

What do you think I should have done? What should I do now?

— *Mom*

DEAR MOM: You sound like a very thoughtful and smart mother. You son wants desperately to understand his own impulses, and he wants just as desperately to keep your high esteem. His actions fall within the normal range for a boy his age. He is curious, and (as you say) his hormones are starting to affect his judgment. This will be the case for a long time.

Talk to him some more about this. Refresh your values and your rules, and tell him that he will face lots of opportunities to make choices — and that you want to help him make good choices.

As he matures, he will be exposed to many temptations — at home, at school and with his friends. That inner voice of his, telling him right from wrong, is the voice he should always listen to. He will make mistakes as he goes, but his honesty and how he handles his mistakes will be the most important determination about the kind of man your boy will grow to become.

Your ongoing attitude toward him should be that you will always be in his corner, prepared to talk about anything — even if it is difficult.